ethical
space

The International Journal
of Communication Ethics

Publishing Office
Abramis Academic
ASK House
Northgate Avenue
Bury St. Edmunds
Suffolk
IP32 6BB
UK

Tel: +44 (0)1284 700321
Fax: +44 (0)1284 717889
Email: info@abramis.co.uk
Web: www.abramis.co.uk

Back issues
Back issues are available
from the Publishers at the
above editorial address.

© 2018 Institute of
Communication Ethics &
Abramis Academic

ISSN 1742-0105
ISBN 978-1-84549-723-1

Printed in the UK.

Aims and scope

Communication ethics is a discipline that supports communication
practitioners by offering tools and analyses for the understanding of
ethical issues. Moreover, the speed of change in the dynamic information
environment presents new challenges, especially for communication
practitioners.

Ethics used to be a specialist subject situated within schools of philosophy.
Today it is viewed as a language and systematic thought process available
to everyone. It encompasses issues of care and trust, social responsibility and
environmental concern and identifies the values necessary to balance the
demands of performance today with responsibilities tomorrow.

For busy professionals, CE is a powerful learning and teaching approach that
encourages analysis and engagement with many constituencies, enhancing
relationships through open-thinking. It can be used to improve organization
performance as well as to protect individual well-being.

Submissions

Papers should be submitted to the Editor via email. Full details on submission –
along with detailed notes for authors – are available online in PDF format:
www.communication-ethics.net

Subscription Information

Each volume contains 4 issues, issued quarterly. Enquiries regarding
subscriptions
and orders both in the UK and overseas should be sent to:

Journals Fulfilment Department
Abramis Academic, ASK House, Northgate Avenue, Bury St. Edmunds,
Suffolk IP32 6BB, UK.
Tel: +44 (0)1284 700321, Fax: +44 (0)1284 717889
Email: info@abramis.co.uk

Your usual suscription agency will also be able to take a subscription to
Ethical Space.

Annual Subscription

Membership of the Institute of Communication Ethics includes a subscription
to the journal. Please see the application form on the last page of this
issue.

For non-members:

Institutional subscription   £200.00
Personal subscription   £55.00

Delivery by surface mail. Airmail prices available on request or at the journal's
web site.

www.communication-ethics.net

ethical
space

The International Journal
of Communication Ethics

Contents

Editorial Board

Filling the ethical vacuum in sports journalism

This special double edition of *Ethical Space* focuses on an often-neglected area of communication ethics: the moral issues surrounding sports journalism. The lack of research and discussion in this area prompted the Institute of Communication Ethics to make sports communication the focus of its annual conference on 27 October 2017. The event, at the Frontline Club in London, had a truly global dimension, with journalists, established sports media academics and postgraduate students attending from the UK, Spain and Australia. The pieces that appear in this issue of *ES* are a consequence of that fruitful conference, which was entitled 'Sports journalism: Ethical vacuum or ethical minefield?'

Should sports journalism have its own bespoke code of conduct and how does regulation affect sports broadcast journalists differently to sports print journalists? How is the ongoing digital revolution affecting the ethical issues confronting sports journalists? To what extent has sports journalism shrugged off its 'toy department' tag? How is clickbait affecting the integrity of sports journalism? Does it make sense to talk of sports journalists having duties, and, if so, to whom? These were just some of the issues raised by the various papers delivered at the conference and which are developed in this edition. But while the papers are varied, there is considerable overlap as key areas fall into focus.

Andy Cairns, executive editor of *Sky Sports News*, who delivered a compelling keynote address, argues in 'Ethical sports journalism – The challenges' that there is a form of self-defeating hypocrisy in sports journalists behaving unethically. Sports journalists hold professional sports people to moral account, criticising them for cheating or for seeking to warp the field of fair contest in any way. And, he argues, if sports journalists hold athletes to that level of ethical scrutiny, then it follows that the journalists themselves should have high moral standards. 'If sports journalists believe in ethical behaviour in the subject we cover,' he writes, 'we, too, should behave ethically.' It could be countered that this equivalence is too simplistic. What if exposing cheating or dishonesty in sport requires reporting techniques that are intuitively ethically questionable, such as clandestine operations or 'door-stepping'? Indeed, Cairns himself acknowledges that the picture is more nuanced, recognising that general principles are easier to identify than the complex decisions of day-to-day sports news gathering in a 24/7 news cycle. However, the underlying point remains – that just as athletes should be 'clean', so should the public expect 'clean news'.

Cairns argues that compliance, adherence to regulation and awareness of codes of conduct are not enough; there needs to be a deeper understanding and appreciation of ethical nuance by his employees and other sports journalists as they face the ethical challenges of sports journalism in 2018. But if codes are not enough in and of themselves, then they are arguably at least a baseline on which the industry can operate. In 'Accountable sports journalism. Building up a platform and a new specialised code in the field', Xavier Ramon-Vegas and José-Luis Rojas-Torrijos argue that the purpose of a bespoke code for the sports journalism industry is two-fold: to raise awareness within the industry of sports journalists' accountability and, secondly, to enhance the public's perception of sports journalists' credibility which, they argue, has been eroded partly by the collapse of the frontier between fact and comment.

In a wide-ranging analysis of the instruments that can hold sports journalists to account, Ramon-Vegas and Rojas-Torrijos illustrate the breadth of codes and other sources of ethical guidance that are in circulation for sports journalists. Their website, *AccountableSportsJournalism.org*, provides a valuable platform which brings together 42 resources from 15 countries in one place. And in their paper they provide their own specialised, 10-point code which, they say, seeks to 'bridge the gap between the ideal and professional practice'. The code is certainly ambitious in scope, not least the section in Clause 7 (Promotion of positive sports values) which asserts that sports journalists 'should contribute to the promotion of positive values, such as... international peace and understanding through their coverage of sports events among citizens, with special attention for youth and children'. While some sports journalists might baulk at the notion of their practice having to adhere to ostensibly political ends, the code is a stimulating decalogue, the final clause of which provides a profound call for a real depth and richness of coverage: 'Sports journalists should go beyond the dramatic action on the field and raise public awareness about relevant contexts that exist behind the play. Sports should be thoroughly explained from their social, financial, cultural and political dimensions.'

Like Cairns, Ramon-Vegas and Rojas-Torrijos recognise that codes are not sufficient in and of themselves to produce ethical sports journalists. As well as being guided by codes and in-house stylebooks, they contend that 'sports journalists must seek ethical guidance from within themselves, by placing emphasis on their individual conscience'. The concept of individual moral agency in sports journalism is explored by Tom Bradshaw, who uses the work of award-winning journalist David Walsh as a means to highlight the tension that exists between professionally pragmatic sports newsgathering techniques and approaches which adhere more strictly to the dictates of duty. Adapting concepts developed by the German philosopher Immanuel Kant, Bradshaw's analysis poses interesting questions about the extent to which sports journalists self-censor, and the way in which certain reporting techniques arguably hinder truthful and accurate reporting.

Bradshaw, an experienced sports journalist as well as an academic, places individual autonomy at the centre of his discussion, and the notion of autonomy is also explored by Simon McEnnis in his examination of the practical impact of codes of conduct on sports journalists' professional conduct. His paper, 'A comparative analysis of how regulatory codes inform broadcast and print sports journalists' work routines in the UK using *Sky Sports News* and the *Sun* as case studies', provides an intricate discussion of what regulation means for sports broadcast journalism versus sports print journalism. McEnnis contends that, while broadcast journalists understand autonomy as freedom from commercial influences, print regulation – as embodied in the Independent Press Standards Organisation's Editors' Code of Practice – is animated by a spirit of ensuring independence from government interference. A central thrust of his paper, informed by his own journalistic experience, is that the routines of TV sports journalists are more influenced by regulatory codes than those of print sports journalists. His conclusion – that, for print journalists, 'freedom of the press means freedom to make unethical deals with corporate organisations' – will no doubt be a trigger for further debate.

Tracie Edmondson, in her paper 'Guess and go': The ethics of mediatisation of professional sport in Australia' develops points made by Cairns and Bradshaw by focusing on how the emergence of the digital 24/7 news cycle has posed new moral dilemmas for sports journalists. Following 26 in-depth, semi-structured interviews with sports communication professionals, her conclusion – that 'routine violations of core ethical standards of Australian journalism' are happening as a consequence of the never-ending digitised sports news cycle – should prompt all connected to the industry to take a step back and consider what ethical sports journalism means in a post-digital revolution landscape. Edmondson's background of 32 years in a range of sports journalism and sports media management roles gives her findings a practical weight, although – as she acknowledges – an interesting counterbalance to the findings would be provided by interviews with Australian sports journalists.

Twitter and other social media platforms have become a vital tool for sports news organisations to reach new audiences, but can the pursuit of audience share compromise quality? As part of a longitudinal analysis examining the Twitter feeds of 15 major football media outlets between 2010 and 2017, Jonathan Cable and Glyn Mottershead conclude that quality is, indeed, being reduced, as outlets pursue 'a never-ending quest for easy content'. In their paper 'Can I click it? Yes you can: Football journalism, Twitter and clickbait', Cable and Mottershead suggest that sports desks and sports journalists should provide more interaction with the audience rather than more clickbait content. 'If the competition is for eyeballs then surely the way to build a community and audience is to interact and not to churn out unsatisfying yet tasty morsels of clickbait for the audience to gorge themselves on.' The question then arises, however, about how an audience so used to a diet of such tasty morsels can be weaned off it.

Charles M. Lambert examines the social media platform from another perspective in 'How to get kicked off Twitter: An examination of the changing ethics of the so-called "tech giants"'. Through case studies looking at two sports journalists whose accounts were taken down by social media companies, Lambert argues that freedom of speech has been undermined by a current focus on tech companies' duty to protect users. In his analysis of the cases of cricket journalist Nishant Joshi and investigative sports reporter Andrew Jennings, Lambert argues that tech companies appear not to have made any attempt to investigate the legitimacy of complaints made against the sports journalists, instead taking down the accounts following mere accusations. Considered alongside Cable and Mottershead's analysis of clickbait, Lambert's paper emphasises the new ethical issues confronting sports journalism practice in the digital age.

It is hoped that this edition of *ES* will serve to stimulate wide-ranging debate about the ethical issues facing sports journalists across the globe in this new digital era. In particular, it is intended that both the conference and this edition of the journal will provide the basis for an on-going partnership between academics and sports journalists in the formulation and exploration of key ethical issues in the industry, enriching the community of sports journalists as a result.

Tom Bradshaw, University of Gloucestershire,
Daragh Minogue, St Mary's University

Ethical sports journalism:
The challenges

Andy Cairns examines some of the many ethical issues facing sports journalists in 2018 and asks: Is it ever legitimate for a sports reporter to behave unethically?

Journalism, sport and ethics – they should go together seamlessly. After all, the purity of sport is one of the reasons we – journalists and fans – are drawn to it. The Olympic ideal talks about a spirit of friendship, solidarity and fair play where universal fundamental ethical principles in sport can make the world a better place.

And while there's an old saying in baseball: 'If you ain't cheating you ain't trying,' most sports make a virtue of virtue. And that's why we watch them, play them and report on them. Indeed, have you ever seen a section of the media harrumph with as much passion and anger as sports journalists when sports people cheat – be that in match-fixing, diving in football or using performance-enhancing drugs to gain an unfair advantage?

Is there a section of the media as outraged as a sports journalist when people in sport maybe play by the rules but against the spirit? So it follows that if sports journalists believe in ethical behaviour in the subject we cover, we should also behave ethically. Especially if the one thing that makes us even angrier than cheating or not playing by the spirit is hypocrisy.

But of course – it's more nuanced than that.

Behaviour

So let's consider: what does an ethical sports news organisation look like, how should ethical sports journalists behave? I like to think that *Sky Sports News* upholds high ethical standards, yet one of our most respected reporters, with our blessing, regularly door-stepped a supposedly frail 70-year-old man, going directly against requests from his family and colleagues. I'll come back to that later.

Andy Cairns

The Leveson Inquiry (2011-2012) brought a sharper focus on ethics and culture across all media. We ensure that everyone at *Sky Sports News* is trained and encouraged to think about ethics. At Sky, our values and our reputation demand it and so do our viewers. And that training should start early.

The pace of news now means journalists are making decisions about what they write, publish and broadcast faster than they have ever done before. As many newsrooms are run with fewer staff, it's very often an inexperienced journalist who will have to make that on-the-spot, instant decision on their own. They need to know what to consider when they make decisions and they need to get it right. They need the right training.

This goes beyond compliance and regulation. Broadcasters work to clear Ofcom guidelines around fairness and privacy that define what we can broadcast and how we treat people when gathering information. So we are heavily regulated already.

Codes of conduct

Most news organisations will have a code of conduct. Point one in ours covers maintaining highest professional and ethical standards and, like other news organisations, it covers areas such as declaring conflict of interest, being fair and accurate, being clear about the distinction between comment, opinion and fact. We also have clear guidelines about not distorting comments or misrepresenting people. And journalists cannot take private advantage of information they learn in their role at *Sky Sports News*.

But compliance, regulations and codes of conduct, while offering some kind of framework don't go anywhere near covering all the ethical challenges a sports journalist faces in 2018. And the role of the sports journalist is changing rapidly.

Maybe unfairly in the past, sports journalists were often accused of being fans with typewriters. There was a feeling they were too close to the players and officials they reported on. They had great access with some great insight and interviews. But were they asking the difficult questions? When news reporters, as opposed to specialist sports reporters, started covering sport they had a greater distance and were able to ask the more difficult questions without worrying about jeopardising relationships.

Some of the greatest resistance to these news journalists covering sport came from old sports hacks. They called them 'the rotters'. But the media explosion since the 1990s has seen a huge change. Sports journalists now are far more rounded. They challenge more and ask tougher questions. But that close relationship has gone. Reporters now very rarely travel with teams. They no longer stay in the same hotels. There aren't the opportunities to go out for a few drinks with a star player, or even meet up for informal chats in hotel bars.

Information and access are strictly controlled by teams of media officers. They dictate who will appear at press conferences. They coach and advise them what to answer and even try to control what questions journalists will ask. Even though I have lived through this change, I'm not sure what came first. Whether the closer journalistic scrutiny led to the more protective environment or whether the more protective environment and tougher access means sports reporters now have a greater distance – and this allows them to step back, take a more critical view and probe more deeply into the broader issues.

Anonymous sources

This attempt to control information by clubs, agents and governing bodies has made it harder for those inside sport who want to speak out. Luckily for journalism, there are still people who do want to talk to journalists. And it has led to the growing phenomenon of the anonymous source.

Journalists, as a rule, will attribute information, quotes and comment. But the people who have the best stories are often also those who have the most to lose if they are discovered. So, reluctantly, we refer to unnamed sources. Where possible we try to give some context by explaining why we have spoken to someone at the highest level at the club, someone with a detailed knowledge of the transfer deal or an insider at whatever governing body. But when we need to protect the identity of the people we refer to them as 'Sky sources'. It's not ideal but it does protect a source while telling our viewers that the information provided is something they can trust.

And not everyone who talks to us is always telling the truth. There are plenty of people eager to give us stories that are untrue. This can range from an agent trying to earn a pay rise for a player by saying another club want to sign him to more elaborate falsehoods and hoaxes.

Trust

Accuracy is important to *Sky Sports News*. Our reputation is built on trust and viewers and readers of our digital products rely on us to get it right. One wrong story can seriously damage our reputation. And often what we don't put to screen is as important, if not more important, than the stories we do run. But with the media explosion over the last few years, it's clear that different rules apply to different organisations.

Andy Cairns

At one end there are the established, trusted services where people come for reliable, quality news. On a smaller scale, the established local and regional papers depend on accuracy for their reputation. If they make mistakes the brand can be severely damaged.

The competition is changing though. We know where we stand with traditional rivals. But there's a disturbing ground occupied by news and gossip sites, sometimes with significant Twitter followings, where different rules apply. They will run stories without checking, will present opinion as fact and run stories that are just wrong. They are popular and they present a problem for traditional news organisations in the battle for viewers and readers.

We've had to respond. Most news organisations followed the 'two sources rule' for any story. With the pace of news and increased competition, that's not workable now, especially as the second source may be trying to break the news themselves on their own website or Twitter feed. So we have a series of checks. Each story is different but our first consideration for story sources who don't want to be named is to challenge whether they are in a position to know for certain.

We also consider our relationship with them and how reliable and trustworthy a contact they are. Then we consider why they are telling us. Any doubt and we keep checking and checking. There's no science to this and we have a fantastic contact base and good systems for quickly standing up and, just as importantly, knocking down stories.

Competition

We also face increasing competition from media organisations with a more cavalier attitude to the truth and to fact-checking, for whom the number of clicks is more important. Official club websites are also desperate to break their good news, in their own way and ahead of established news organisations. They want to announce new signings, control the questions and the answers on interviews.

We have also had to react to the number of rumours on social media. We have set up a special news team whose first priority is to break original news but, as a secondary role, it checks out, quickly and reliably, some of the wilder stories originating on social media. Because of our scale, our contacts and our reputation, we can very quickly establish when a rumour has something in it and we can also knock down a rumour very quickly when there's nothing in it.

The challenge comes when a rumour gathers significant momentum on social media. We can't ignore it so we tell our viewers that this is a rumour we know is gaining traction, that we are checking to verify and that we will update as soon as we can. It's not where we were a few years ago, where we waited to confirm a story before putting it to air, but it's being honest with our audience.

Theft
So checking content is important. Responsible media organisations will invest in journalism but they are facing a new threat from ripping and piracy. Both are theft. Piracy is illegal, unreliable and harmful. Greater emphasis has been placed on the commercial impact than the ethical but both are important. And are linked. Enforcement agencies are now cracking down on piracy and those who sell illegal streams are going to jail.

And there are ethical issues. If you are paying for a stream from someone who has accessed it illegally you would wonder what ethical code they operate under. There's no protection for children, no protection from malicious software which could expose people to theft of personal data and financial scams.

This isn't just about Sky, or solely about sport. It goes beyond both. Millions of people are employed in the creative economy and piracy puts those jobs at risk. We invest heavily to bring paying customers the best in sport content and news. Those who are paying legally are subsidising those who don't. Indeed, if more people were paying then the cost could come down.

Then there's the issue around ripping. Gathering and producing news is hard work. It takes skill, perseverance and professionalism. It costs. But more and more sites are ripping and lifting content with no journalism of their own. No checks, no attempt to develop the story.

Any newsroom anywhere when it sees a good story elsewhere will try to follow it up. At *Sky Sports News*, we hate being beaten to a story but it happens. And when it happens we work hard to take ownership of that story. First step is to verify and confirm the story first hand. And then we look for new lines to move the story on.

What we find unethical is other sites, and it's mainly on digital media, lifting stories, video, graphics, data and research and publishing them without any checks. So for *Sky Sports News*, trust is important. All our research shows that viewers and readers trust us as a reliable news service. That brings responsibilities and challenges. Rolling news puts huge pressures on journalists and means we rarely have time to stand back and look at the bigger picture. But we should.

Responsible reporting
Sports journalists now regularly cover issues that shine a light on some of the key ethical questions in the broader society. Over the

Andy Cairns

last year sports writers have covered stories about race and sex discrimination, corruption, gambling, drugs, abuse and mental health. The industry needs journalists equipped to handle these questions. And, as we look at these issues, it follows that we should look at the way we gather and present news.

The British Psychological Society has raised awareness around the use of language and the impact of irresponsible reporting around mental health.[1] And sports journalists have challenged the tone of reporting especially after mental health has become such an issue in sport. MIND, the mental health charity, has published research which shows that people aged between 16-34 have a one-in-four chance of meeting the clinical criteria for one or more mental health disorders.[2] That age range just about captures an athlete's career span. So just think about the challenges they face: a 16-year-old footballer, moving away from home to a new environment facing isolation, to someone in their mid-30s with their career coming to an end, facing rejection, being dropped, sold to a lesser club and their status diminished.

And during their career, constantly under scrutiny from coaches, from fans on social media and from sports journalists and pundits assessing their performance. The mental health of a player is the responsibility of their employers. But we in the media must be aware of our responsibilities too and the ethical issues around reporting mental health.

At *Sky Sports News*, we run training courses, invite guest speakers from MIND and players who have suffered from mental health issues. We need to keep learning about how we best report these issues and to help people who watch, listen and read our content to achieve a better understanding.

Clean news

So how we present news and how we gather news bring us challenges. Sports journalism is competitive. We go head-to-head each day with rivals for viewers and eyeballs. Chasing accurate, reliable information and beating the competition gets harder. But in the way sports fans expect players to win clean, so our viewers and readers expect us to be clean in our news gathering. They have to trust that we are finding and reporting sports news in the right way.

It's something we take incredibly seriously. And it makes sense on so many levels. After all, the bigger the story, the bigger chance it will involve someone rich, powerful, clever and with access to expensive lawyers.

If we don't behave ethically there's a danger attention is focused on the way we gathered the story rather than the story itself. So is it ever right to go against your code, to behave unethically, when chasing a story? I mentioned earlier that one of our reporters door-stepped a supposedly frail, 70-year-old man against his wishes and those of his colleagues. It's something we discussed and decided we felt we had to do.

You may be thinking: 'That's odd – why would they do that when they harp on about ethical behaviour?' Well, the 70-year-old man in question was Sepp Blatter who, at the time, was head of FIFA, the international football association. Ofcom guidelines say door-stepping can be used when there are repeated refusals to grant an interview. Well, Mr Blatter would often hold press conferences but these are tactical battles now and carefully orchestrated by PR people. They may seem to be open and the interviewee looks as though they are answering questions but the reality is different.

KEYNOTE
TALK

Through a mixture of time-wasting, not answering the question that's been asked, not allowing follow-up questions, providing carefully rehearsed answers, interrupting any fluency from the floor, making sure the interviewee goes back to the 'safe house' answer at every opportunity, it is all a charade. It gives the appearance of an open press conference but, in reality, is anything but.

At the time, Blatter had big questions to answer. We knew we could find ways to get to him but that also brings up ethical questions. We could have asked security staff, chauffeurs and doormen who could tell us which car he had been in and which door he would be leaving by. But they could have lost their jobs if their employers found out they had talked to us.

Sometimes, though, people are willing to help. We found which door he had been leaving his hotel by and which car he'd be getting in. We door-stepped and chased Blatter in the street, asked him some questions, received some great answers and had an exclusive which was picked up by rivals and shone a touch more light on the darker goings on at FIFA at the time.

As news gathering gets harder the role of the sports journalist is changing. So is there a formula for what is right, is it ever appropriate for sports journalists to behave unethically? I am excited that there is now a big debate going on, that sports journalists are more aware of ethical issues, how they are distinct from regulation and compliance, how they affect the way we work every day. It's a debate that's been evolving and one that needs to continue if sports journalism is to prosper in the years ahead.

Notes

1 http://thepsychologist.bps.org.uk/volume-30/august-2017/when-winners-need-help, accessed on 6 January 2018

Andy Cairns

2 https://www.mind.org.uk/information-support/types-of-mental-health-problems/statistics-and-facts-about-mental-health/how-common-are-mental-health-problems/#.WlTdUvll_IU, accessed on 6 January 2018

Note on the contributor

Andy Cairns is Executive Editor at *Sky Sports News*, overseeing a team of around 200 sports journalists producing sports news across Sky's digital and TV platforms. He has been a journalist for almost 40 years. He is a board member and trustee of the National Council for the Training of Journalists where he also chairs the Accreditation Board. He acted as an adviser on the Women and Sport Advisory Board for the Digital, Culture, Media and Sport select committee in 2015.

Xavier Ramon-Vegas
José-Luis Rojas-Torrijos

Accountable sports journalism. Building up a platform and a new specialised code in the field

Far from its traditional consideration as the 'little brother' of the profession, sports journalism plays a key role in the new information ecosystem and has a huge impact in society. Therefore, sports journalists must gain awareness of their accountability in order to counteract the widespread deficiencies that have not only challenged the normative standards of the profession but have also eroded their credibility. With the aim of helping journalists address these shortcomings, this investigation: (1) has compiled and examined the most relevant ethical codes, stylebooks and other accountability instruments in sports journalism; (2) has created the online platform Accountable Sports Journalism (http://accountablesportsjournalism.org); and (3) has produced a new specialised code aimed at covering sports responsibly.

Key words: accountability, code, ethics, instruments, sports journalism

In the current cluttered and 'increasingly complex digital media landscape' (Boyle and Haynes 2014: 85), sport content is 'available from a growing range of digital, mobile media and telecommunications companies and intermediaries' (Hutchins and Boyle 2017: 505) as well as from communication departments at clubs and leagues (Suggs 2016). For legacy media, despite its 'perennial dismissal as trivial subject matter' (Weedon et al. 2016: 1), sport remains a pivotal asset to attract advertisers and audiences (Hutchins and Rowe 2009).

In this context of 'digital plenitude' (Hutchins and Rowe 2009), sports journalists face severe challenges, including 'commercial and economic restrictions' (English 2017: 534), 'greater demands in terms of publishing platforms, technology, content and workloads'

Xavier
Ramon-Vegas
José-Luis
Rojas-Torrijos

(English 2016: 1002) and 'growing competition from content aggregators and "social" news specialists' (Hutchins and Boyle 2017: 499). Professionals also struggle with the seemingly endless growth of the PR industry in the world of sport (L'Etang 2013; Sherwood, Nicholson and Marjoribanks 2017).

However, as Hutchins and Boyle (2017: 497) highlight, 'the influence of multiple crosscutting forces does not mean that shared practices of news work no longer exist, or that journalists have voluntarily ceded their cultural authority to "the crowd" in determining what counts as news and how it should be produced and delivered'. Beyond adapting their skills 'to meet the demands of a converged media environment' (Ketterer, McGuire and Murray 2014: 282), sports journalists should maintain the essential principles of ethics at the core of their professional task (Oates and Pauly 2007). Ethics and accountability should be at the centre stage of the 'community of practice' of sports journalism. This is essential to counteract the widespread deficiencies that have not only challenged the normative standards of the profession but have also eroded the credibility and status of its professionals (Horky and Stelzner 2013).

'The toy department': Exploring the ethical shortcomings in sports journalism
Sports journalism has been labelled as the 'toy department' or the 'sandbox' of the newsroom (Rowe 2007). Its professionals 'have been described as cheerleaders, hero worshippers, fans, homers and sycophants' and as 'biased and responsible for boosterism of athletes, teams, organisations and the sports industry' (English 2017: 532). The dissolution of the frontiers between facts and comments has been commonplace in the field (Boyle 2006). Rumour and speculation have pervaded the coverage, which has also been 'subordinated to entertainment as a way of expression incorporating sensationalist elements that come from the spectacle industries' (Rojas-Torrijos 2011: 18). The use of violence metaphors and images in sports reporting, connected to 'commodification of sport, and its marketing as spectacle' (Holt 2000: 102) has also been frequent.

The limited range of sources has been mainly drawn 'from the ranks of celebrity athletes, coaches and administrators, thus further isolating the sports desk from the world beyond sport' (Rowe 2007: 400-401). Partly because of this interplay between media and the sport industry, sports journalists have failed to cover properly the 'problems, issues and topics that permeate the social world to which sport is intimately connected' (Rowe 2007: 400). Thus, they have proved unable to comply with the essential 'watchdog' and investigative functions of journalism in democratic societies. There are some noteworthy exceptions to this trend, such as the broader perspective shown by US newspapers in the coming out of Jason

Collins and Michael Sam (Cassidy 2017); the critical reports in the Australia–India Test cricket series (English 2017); the exposure of child abuse in football (Taylor 2017); the investigation of corruption cases at FIFA (Jennings 2011) or the research on Lance Armstrong, pursued by David Walsh of *The Sunday Times* and the blog *NYVelocity* (Brock 2013). Yet, the amount of critical interrogation on the world of sport is scant compared to other genres.

In addition, as Suggs (2016: 265) highlights, 'news coverage looks surprisingly uniform across different publications and different media'. Moreover, sportswomen, non-white and impaired athletes have been marginalised in the coverage (O'Neill and Mulready 2015; Tulloch and Ramon-Vegas 2017) and have been often presented through the lens of stereotypes. To illustrate, in their recent examination of the US press coverage of Alex Rodriguez, the baseball player, for his alleged use of performance-enhancing drugs, Brennen and Brown (2016: 29) found that newspapers 'dehumanized Rodriguez through repeated use of overtly racist and animalistic imagery'.

The role of accountability instruments in sports journalism
To mitigate the long-held claims of sports journalism being a 'bastion of easy living, sloppy journalism and "soft" news' (Boyle 2006: 1), 'sports journalists must also be accountable to the professional norms that advance the entire profession's credibility' (Hardin and Zhong 2010: 6). The concept of accountability refers to 'the commitment of media organisations and professionals to be held accountable by society for their practices' (Rojas-Torrijos and Ramon-Vegas 2017: 916). According to McQuail (2003: 19), 'accountable communication exists where authors (originators, sources, or gatekeepers) take responsibility for the quality and consequences of their publication, orient themselves to audiences and others affected, and respond to their expectations and those of the wider society'. Traditional and innovative media accountability instruments (Bertrand 2000) – including ethical codes, stylebooks, recommendations issued by organisations, ombudsmen websites and scholars' or citizens' blogs – can play major roles in offering guidance and helping journalists and users monitor and assess the quality of sports content (Ramon-Vegas and Rojas-Torrijos 2017).

Objective and methodology
Taking the aforementioned framework into account, the objective of this research has been to compile, examine and disseminate the most relevant accountability instruments in sports journalism. The first stage of the project involved mapping and analysing the most relevant instruments in the field. We first monitored the internet over an 18-month period (October 2015-March 2017) to locate the most relevant instruments across different countries, media systems and journalistic cultures. Through snowball sampling, the

Xavier
Ramon-Vegas
José-Luis
Rojas-Torrijos

instruments were identified and progressively incorporated into the sample. Afterwards, the researchers examined each one of those instruments using the qualitative content analysis technique (Bryman 2016). The categories of the analysis included the following: instruments produced inside or outside of media organisations, description of the specifications for and use of the instruments, and evaluation of the mechanisms from the accountability perspective (Ramon-Vegas and Rojas-Torrijos 2017).

The second stage of the research involved the creation, in April 2017, of the platform *Accountable Sports Journalism* (*http://accountablesportsjournalism.org*) to make the instruments readily accessible to media practitioners, scholars and students. On this site, users can find access to the instruments produced inside the media (in-house stylebooks promoted by major sports media, recommendations for sports journalists in news agencies and general information outlets, ombudsmen and online chats) and to tools implemented outside media companies (external codes, recommendations issued by key stakeholders in the world of sport, the largest publications related to media criticism, as well as several scholars' and citizens' blogs). The range of resources on the platform is being enhanced on an on-going basis. Nowadays, *Accountable Sports Journalism* brings together 42 resources (*n=42*) from 15 different countries, along with those produced by international organisations. Finally, after critically examining all the instruments available, the investigation has produced a new specialised code in sports journalism ('Guidelines for covering sports responsibly').

Results
Accountability instruments on a new platform
So far, 42 accountability instruments have been located and uploaded on to the *Accountable Sports Journalism* platform. Those have been classified, as previously noted, into two categories: instruments produced within media organisations and those created outside of them.

Instruments produced inside media companies or media groups
Stylebooks and guidelines promoted by major sports media
One of the fundamental accountability instruments is in-house stylebooks which establish an implicit contract between journalists and citizens. One of the scarce sports outlets that has adapted its stylebook to the digital environment is *Bleacher Report* (*http://bleacherreport.com/pages/styleguide*). Another American outlet concerned with accountability is *ESPN*, which has published its *Editorial guidelines for standards & practices* (*http://edge-cache.deadspin.com/deadspin/editorial.pdf*). As their authors note, the purpose of the editorial guidelines 'is the protection of *ESPN*'s journalistic credibility across all platforms'. These recommendations

tackle a wide range of ethical issues, including: transparency, commentary, sourcing, attribution, corrections, media criticism, activity on social networking sites and advertising. *Grantland*, a sports and culture website created by Bill Simmons in 2011 and discontinued in 2015, developed useful terminological glossaries on sports like tennis, wrestling, basketball, American football and baseball (*http://grantland.com/tags/grantland-dictionary/*).

Recommendations for sports coverage proposed by agencies and general information outlets
News agencies and general information outlets worldwide have also proposed recommendations for sports journalists. In Europe, the *Reuters sports style guide* (*http://handbook.reuters.com/ index.php?title=Sports_Style_Guide*) is one of the key documents available. In Spain, the major public broadcasting corporations have specific sections devoted to sports in their in-house handbooks: namely *RTVE*, the Spanish public broadcasting corporation (*http:// manualdeestilo.rtve.es/*); *CCMA*, the Catalan Corporation of Audiovisual Media (*http://www.ccma.cat/llibredestil/*) and *Canal Sur*, the radio and TV corporation in Andalusia. In complying with their remit as public service broadcasters (PSBs), these institutions stress the importance of disseminating the positive values associated with sport.

Moving on to America, the *Ethical journalism handbook* from *The New York Times* (*https://www.nytco.com/wp-content/uploads/ NYT_Ethical_Journalism_0904-1.pdf*) outlines three rules (131-333) addressed to the sports desk. More precisely, it mentions that journalists should avoid gambling on sports events and serving as scorers and that they should not 'accept tickets, travel expenses, meals, gifts or any other benefit from teams or promoters'. Further references to conflicts of interest are included in documents issued by *Minnesota Public Radio* (*http://www.mpr.org/about/news_ ethics*) and the *Los Angeles Times* (*http://latimesblogs.latimes. com/readers/2011/02/la-times-ethics-guidelines.html*). Conversely, other news organisations such as the *Columbia Missourian* (*http://convergence.journalism.missouri.edu/wp-content/ uploads/2009/04/missourian-stylebook.pdf*) focus on providing guidance on sports language.

Online ombudsmen/ombudswomen
The role of ombudsmen/ombudswomen is nearly non-existent in sports media outlets. The exception can be found in *ESPN*'s public editor, a pioneering post created in 2005 to ensure that the content of the network complies with its *Editorial guidelines*. The public editor (*http://espn.go.com/blog/ombudsman*) fosters transparency and helps fans understand *ESPN*'s journalistic culture and the editorial criteria behind the content. He writes a monthly column, reflecting on core aspects such as the loosening of standards

Xavier Ramon-Vegas

José-Luis Rojas-Torrijos

with the treatment of *ESPN* Body Issue photographs, the use of sponsored content, the criteria employed by the company to select their anchors or the debates about conflict of interest.

Online chats
Online chats, which help foster live interaction between readers, editorial teams and experts, have expanded in recent years and have proved to be powerful tools for discussing editorial criteria and handling errors (Rojas-Torrijos and Ramon-Vegas 2017). *ESPN*'s programme *Sportsnation* has promoted live chats since 2008. All the live conversations *(http://espn.go.com/sportsnation/chat/ archive)* can be retrieved at any time from *ESPN*'s website.

Instruments produced outside media companies or groups
Specialised codes in sports journalism
The range of external codes devoted exclusively to sports journalism is fairly limited. The most recognised document is the *Ethics guidelines* promoted by the Associated Press Sports Editors (APSE) *(http://apsportseditors.com/apse-ethics-guidelines/)*. The code, created in 1974 and revised in 1991, is built around seven cornerstones that urge journalists to safeguard professional independence, verify information, be attentive to sources and avoid gender and race discrimination. In 2014, the International Sports Press Association (AIPS) approved its *Code of professional conduct*. The document *(http://www.aipsmedia.com/acopcs/AIPS_CODE_ OF_PROFESSIONAL_CONDUCT_STANDARDS.pdf)*, provides 13 guiding principles, including the need to be knowledgeable about the law, work with honesty and integrity, provide information about potential conflicts of interest, correct errors and avoid publishing false information. In addition, professionals are reminded about their duty to update their knowledge.

The Football Writers Association of America (FWAA) provides recommendations in four areas: the search for truth, minimising harm, professional independence and accountability *(http://www. sportswriters.net/fwaa/about/ethics.html)*. The ethical code of the Automobile Journalists Association of Canada (AJAC) also considers the avoidance of any conflict of interest a cornerstone *(http://www. ajac.ca/web/about/ethics.asp)*. The American Auto Racing Writers & Broadcasters Association (AARWBA) has its own code: *The white paper (http://www.aarwba.org/aarwbawp.htm)*.

In the European context, we should highlight the *Italian media and sports code (http://ethicnet.uta.fi/italy/media_and_sports_code)*. This code is organised in six chapters that seek to promote justice, dignity and the citizens' right to receive information. Moreover, the eight guidelines presented in 2010 by the German association of sports journalists, the *Verband Deutscher Sportjournalisten (http:// www.sportjournalist.de/Ueber_uns/Leitlinien/)* are noteworthy.

20   Vol 15, No 1/2 2018

These recommendations emphasise the public function of sports journalism and call for non-discrimination. The *VDS* also highlights the importance of maintaining independence, respecting individuals' privacy and ensuring accuracy (Horky and Stelzer 2013). In eastern European countries, there's the Serbian Sports Journalists Association (USNS) *Code and sport journalists' club ethics (http://www.usns.rs/wp-content/uploads/2016/10/Kodeks-sportskih-novinara-Srbije.pdf)* and the *Moral code (http://www.ksn.cz/o-ksn/eticky-a-moralni-kodex)* from the Czech Republic. Both are concise texts focused on standards such as safeguarding independence and verifying information.

There are other relevant codes in Latin America: the *Sports Journalists Association ethics code* (Puerto Rico) *(http://www.wallice.com/apdpur/reglamento.html)*, *Manual de Conduta Ética* da Associaçao Brasiliense de Cronistas Desportivos (ABCD) (Brazil) *(http://abcdesportes.com.br/abcd/manual-de-conduta-etica-da-abcd/)* and the Argentinian Federation of Sports Journalists (FAPED) *Ethics code (https://web.archive.org/web/20160328143342/http://faped.org/estatutos.html)*.

General codes of media ethics
In addition to specialised codes in sports, professionals can consult the website *Accountable Journalism (http://accountablejournalism.org/)* created by the Donald W. Reynolds Journalism Institute at the University of Missouri. The site contains more than 400 general and specialised deontological codes from around the world. Among them, central documents such as UNESCO's *International principles of professional ethics (http://ethicnet.uta.fi/international/international_principles_of_professional_ethics_in_journalism)*, the International Federation of Journalists' (IFJ) *Declaration of principles on the conduct of journalists (http://www.ifj.org/about-ifj/ifj-code-of-principles/)* and the Society of Professional Journalists' *Code of ethics (https://www.spj.org/ethicscode.asp)* should be highlighted.

Recommendations for sports journalists issued by key stakeholders
Recommendations issued by key stakeholders in the world of sport should also be taken into account. Among those suggestions, two relevant ones are accessible online: the *Code of sports ethics*, from the Council of Europe *(https://rm.coe.int/16805cecaa)* and the *Charte d'etique et de déontologie du sport Français* (CNOSF 2012). Both emphasise the media's responsibility to promote fair play and set a positive example to children and young people. Moreover, the *Code of sports ethics*, devised by the Portuguese Institute for Sport and Youth *(http://www.pned.pt/media/31485/Code-of-Sports-Ethics.pdf)*, includes a section on recommendations with regard to objectivity, truth and privacy.

**Xavier
Ramon-Vegas
José-Luis
Rojas-Torrijos**

In addition, the International Paralympic Committee (2014) created an 18-page document entitled *Guide to reporting on persons with an impairment*. This easy-to-use guide provides journalists with general rules and a list of preferred terminology and incorrect terms. Similarly, in 2012 the British Paralympic Association published *Guide to reporting on paralympic sport*, (*http://paralympics.org. uk/uploads/documents/ParalympicsGB_Guide_to_Reporting_on_ Paralympic_Sport.pdf*). The Special Olympics (2014) *Style guide* is also available to practitioners.

Other external recommendations
Recommendations also come from institutions that promote the appropriate use of language, such as Fundación del Español Urgente (Fundéu), created in 2005 by the news agency EFE and BBVA with the support of the Royal Spanish Academy (RAE). In 2013, Fundéu created a specific section on the language of football, entitled 'Liga BBVA del Español Urgente' (*http://www. fundeu.es/especiales/liga-del-espanol-urgente/*). Recommendations for the whole sports community are included in *Violence in sport* (*http://www.consejoaudiovisualdeandalucia.es/sites/default/files/ recomendaciones/Recomendaciones_2009_01_Violencia%20 deporte.pdf*), a document jointly produced in 2009 by the Andalusian Audiovisual Council and the regional Federation of Sports Journalists (FPDA).

Media observatories and specialised publications in media criticism
Although there is a lack of observatories exclusively devoted to sports journalism, the largest publications related to media criticism around the world examine the good and bad practices of sports media. A relevant example here is *Ética Segura*, a site created by Fundación Nuevo Periodismo Iberoamericano (Colombia), which regularly promotes debates about ethical issues in the sports field (*http://www.fnpi.org/es/keywords/prensa-deportiva*).

Scholars' and citizens' blogs
Finally, other innovative instruments such as scholars' and citizens' blogs also promote reflection on news quality. In Spain, we highlight *La Buena Prensa* (*http://labuenaprensa. blogspot.com.es/*) and *Periodismo Deportivo de Calidad* (*http:// periodismodeportivodecalidad.blogspot.com.es/*). In the United States, two key examples should be considered: the blogs from the National Sports Journalism Center at Indiana University (*http:// sportsjournalism.org/*) and the Center for Journalism Ethics at the University of Wisconsin-Madison (*http://ethics.journalism.wisc. edu/*).

Creating a new specialised code in the field
Bearing in mind that 'sports journalism should not be exempt from scrutiny regarding conventional professional criteria within the news

arena' (Rowe 2007: 386), researchers examined all the materials included in *Accountable Sports Journalism* to produce a new ethical code, named 'Guidelines for covering sports responsibly' (*https://accountablesportsjournalism.org/code/*). In order to bridge the gap between the ideal and professional practice and to encourage journalists to use such guidelines, these have been kept as short and operational as possible. The Decalogue, which was first presented in October 2017 at the annual conference of the Institute of Communication Ethics ('Sports journalism: Ethical vacuum or ethical minefield?'), in London, presents the following points:

1. Public function and right to sports information
Sports journalists should report on all areas of sport. As an essential part of their public-service approach, they should not only concentrate on mainstream disciplines but also give exposure to underrepresented sports that generate news and have a large number of practitioners. This can help to broaden the coverage and expand citizens' sporting culture. Media professionals should not report on the private lives of sports people unless the information is relevant to understanding the athletes' performance.

PAPER

2. Conflict of interest
Sports journalists should avoid taking part in activities that lie outside of their professional realm or in employment that may create conflict of interest. This includes working in the field of public relations (PR) and as advisors for a sports person, club or federation, and writing for a team or league publication. Editors and reporters cannot be sources who are assigned to themselves. Behaving professionally entails remaining loyal to the news organisation for which one works.

3. Hospitality from sources and independence
Sports journalists should reject invitations and gifts from teams or promoters that could call into question their working as independent eyewitnesses. Likewise, they should not use their position as journalists to obtain free tickets for any sports event from sources other than those which customarily make passes or tickets available when a performance has a clear bearing on the journalist's job.

4. Newsgathering and impartiality
Sports journalists should avoid developing a close relationship with sports sources and maintain a critical distance by seeking and using a varied and representative number of arguments and facts on any issue, and presenting them appropriately without bias towards their audiences. They should also avoid misconduct such as 'boosterism' and nationalistic or chauvinistic approaches. Impartiality entails being professional rather than behaving like fans.

Xavier Ramon-Vegas

José-Luis Rojas-Torrijos

5. Factual reporting

Sports journalists are committed to truthful and factual reporting. They should establish a clear distinction between facts and their personal opinions about them, as well as between news and advertising or sponsored content. Reinforcing methods of verification is essential to the fight against fake news, the pervasiveness of speculation and rumour in sports content, and to discarding sensationalism and trivialisation in news reporting.

6. Journalistic quality and use of language

Sports journalists are committed to journalistic quality and must, therefore, rely on a correct use of language as their main working tool to enhance their stories. Acquiring a vast vocabulary and developing the ability to use suitable words and phrases in referring to any sportsperson are valuable assets towards improving content quality within the field.

7. Promotion of positive sports values

Sports journalists should contribute to the promotion of positive values, such as fair play, non-discrimination and international peace and understanding through their coverage of sports events among citizens, with special attention for youth and children.

8. Violence in sports

Sports journalists must avoid using warlike language, as well as disseminating expressions and images that emphasise or legitimate any form of violence towards individuals or groups of people within or outside sports venues. Sport is not a substitute for war. Thus, journalists must minimise confrontational narratives and warlike imagery.

9. Gender perspective

To counteract the long-standing under-representation of sportswomen, sports journalists should work with greater dedication to promote equality in their reporting by giving female athletes more exposure when their results deserve it. More women should be incorporated as expert sources into the news agenda. Sexist comments and stereotypes should be avoided when referring to them.

10. Sports beyond sports

Sports journalists should go beyond the dramatic action on the field and raise public awareness about relevant contexts that exist behind the play. Sports should be thoroughly explained from their social, financial, cultural and political dimensions.

This text is not intended to be read in isolation. Sports journalists should also observe the general principles of trustfulness, fairness, social responsibility and respect for the universal values and diversity of cultures that are included in the baseline codes of the profession. These codes are the UNESCO's *International principles of professional ethics in journalism*, the International Federation of Journalists' (IFJ) *Declaration of principles on the conduct of journalists* and further documents available on *https://accountablejournalism. org/ethics-codes*. Beyond these general and specific codes, as well as their organisations' in-house guidelines, sports journalists must seek ethical guidance from within themselves, by placing emphasis on their individual conscience.

Conclusion

As outlined at the beginning of this paper, many interlinked factors, constraints, debates and tensions contribute to the quality of the media's output in the contemporary 'fluid and commercially volatile context' (Hutchins and Boyle 2017: 496). That being said, sports journalism is a very important commercial engine for newspapers and, therefore, its task should be guided by the same professional values, ethical standards and demands for quality that apply to all journalism. The escalating pressures, orientation towards the market and the tensions of immediacy in this high-speed media landscape should not deter journalists from pursuing the goal of an ethical and comprehensive treatment of sports that ultimately links to media's public service mission in democratic societies.

PAPER

Weedon and Wilson (2017: 22) pose the following question: 'Could sports journalism (and its educative forms) in the future inherit more from the idealist's vision of journalism as a democratic project intended for the betterment of society, than from the allure and prestige of covering sports?' In the light of this question, we contend that all the actors involved in the communicative process (media organisations, citizens and researchers) are responsible in promoting accountability in sports journalism. With the aim of contributing to this task, this investigation has located, examined and made available to professionals, scholars and citizens the most relevant accountability instruments in this field, stemming from different countries and journalistic cultures around the world. Even though there are differences in the ethical practices of sports journalists 'based at least partly on the expectations and cultures within their beats' (Hardin and Zhong 2010: 9), the resources available in the *Accountable Sports Journalism* platform, as well as the 'Guidelines for covering sports responsibly' code, can help current and future practitioners around the globe to be better equipped to develop their task.

To capture an even greater idea of accountability in sports journalism, further work should be carried out. Following the international approach employed so far, future research must track and thoroughly examine the new accountability instruments that emerge in the field. Drawing on these new contributions, which will

Xavier
Ramon-Vegas
José-Luis
Rojas-Torrijos

be progressively incorporated into *Accountable Sports Journalism*, the proposed guidelines will be updated to point journalists in the right direction with regard to language and the highest reporting standards. To maximise the transference of knowledge of the project, the authors will also present the platform and its code to professional associations, media organisations and higher education institutions in different countries.

References

Bertrand, Claude-Jean (2000) *Media ethics and accountability systems*, London, Transaction Publishers

Boyle, Raymond (2006) *Sports journalism: Context and issues*, London, Sage

Boyle, Raymond and Haynes, Richard (2014) Watching the games, Girginov, Vassil (ed.) *Handbook of the London 2012 Olympic and Paralympic Games, Vol. 2*, Abingdon, Routledge pp 84-95

Brennen, Bonnie and Brown, Rick (2016) Persecuting Alex Rodriguez: Race, money and the ethics of reporting the performance-enhancing drug scandal, *Journalism Studies*, Vol. 17, No. 1 pp 21-38

Brock, George (2013) *Out of print. Newspapers, journalism and the business of news in the digital age*, London, Kogan Page

Bryman, Alan (2016) *Social research methods*, Oxford, Oxford University Press, fifth edition

Cassidy, William P. (2017) Inching away from the toy department, *Communication & Sport*, Vol. 5, No. 5 pp 534-553

CNOSF (2012) Charte d'etique et déontologie du sport Français. Available online at http://franceolympique.com/files/File/publications/Charte%20ethique%20 et%20de%20deontologie%20du%20sport%20adoptee%20par%20AG%20 CNOSF%202012.05.10.pd

English, Peter (2016) Mapping the sports journalism field: Bourdieu and broadsheet newsrooms, *Journalism*, Vol. 17, No. 8 pp 1001-1017

English, Peter (2017) Cheerleaders or critics? Australian and Indian sports journalists in the contemporary age, *Digital Journalism*, Vol. 5, No. 5 pp 532-548

Hardin, Marie and Zhong, Bu (2010) Sports reporters' attitudes about ethics vary based on beat, *Newspaper Research Journal*, Vol. 31, No. 2 pp 6-19

Holt, Ron (2000) The discourse ethics of sports print journalism, *Culture, Sport, Society*, Vol. 3, No 3 pp 88-103

Horky, Thomas and Stelzner, Barbara (2013) Sports reporting and journalistic principles, Pedersen, Paul M. (ed.) *Routledge handbook of sport communication*, Abingdon, Routledge pp 118-127.

Hutchins, Brett and Rowe, David (2009) From broadcast scarcity to digital plenitude: The changing dynamics of the media sport content economy, *Television & New Media*, Vol. 10, No. 4 pp 354-370

Hutchins, Brett and Boyle, Raymond (2017) A community of practice: Sport journalism, mobile media and institutional change, *Digital Journalism*, Vol. 5, No. 5 pp 496-512

International Paralympic Committee (2014) Guide to reporting on persons with an impairment. Available online at https://www.paralympic.org/sites/default/files/docu ment/141027103527844_2014_10_31+Guide+to+reporting+on+persons+with+a n+impairment.pdf

Ketterer, Stan, McGuire, John and Murray, Ray (2014) Contrasting desired sports journalism skills in a convergent media environment, *Communication and Sport*, Vol. 2, No 3 pp 282-298

Jennings, Andrew (2011) Investigating corruption in corporate sport: The IOC and FIFA, *International Review for the Sociology of Sport*, Vol. 46, No. 4 pp 387-398

L'Etang, Jacquie (2013) *Sports public relations*, London, Sage

McQuail, Denis (2003) *Media accountability and freedom of publication*, New York, Oxford University Press

Oates, Thomas P. and Pauly, John (2007) Sports journalism as moral and ethical discourse, *Journal of Mass Media Ethics*, Vol. 22, No. 4 pp 332-347

O'Neill, Deirdre and Mulready, Matt (2015) The invisible woman? *Journalism Practice*, Vol. 9, No. 5 pp 651-668

Ramon-Vegas, Xavier and Rojas, José Luis (2017) Mapping media accountability instruments in sports journalism, *El Profesional de la Información*, Vol. 26, No. 2 pp 159-171

Rojas-Torrijos, José Luis (2011) *Periodismo deportivo de calidad: propuesta de un modelo de libro de estilo panhispánico para informadores deportivos*, Madrid, Fragua

Rojas-Torrijos, José Luis and Ramon-Vegas, Xavier (2017) Accountability in social networks. Ever-evolving stylebooks and feedback through Twitter, *Revista Latina de Comunicación Social*, No. 72 pp 915-941

Rowe, David (2007) Sports journalism: Still the 'toy department' of the news media? *Journalism*, Vol. 8, No. 4 pp 385-405

Sherwood, Merryn, Nicholson, Matthew and Marjoribanks, Timothy (2017) Controlling the message and the medium?: The impact of sports organisations' digital and social channels on media access, *Digital Journalism*, Vol. 5, No. 5 pp 513-531

Special Olympics (2014) Special Olympics style guide. Available online at http://media.specialolympics.org/soi/files/resources/Communications/StyleGuide-2014.pdf

Suggs, David Welch (2016) Tensions in the press box, *Communication & Sport*, Vol. 4, No. 3 pp 261-281

Taylor, Daniel (2017) One year after football's child abuse scandal broke, stories are yet to be told, *Observer*, 11 November. Available online at https://www.theguardian.com/football/2017/nov/11/andy-woodward-one-year-on

Tulloch, Christopher and Ramon-Vegas, Xavier (2017) Take five: How *Sports Illustrated* and *L'Équipe* redefine the long form sports journalism genre, *Digital Journalism*, Vol. 5, No. 5 pp 652-672

Weedon, Gavin and Wilson, Brian (2017) Textbook journalism? Objectivity, education and the professionalization of sports reporting, *Journalism* pp 1-26. Available online at http://journals.sagepub.com/doi/abs/10.1177/1464884917716503?journalCode=joua

Weedon, Gavin, Wilson, Brian, Yoon, Liv and Lawson, Shawna (2016) Where's all the 'good' sports journalism? Sports media research, the sociology of sport, and the question of quality sports reporting, *International Review for the Sociology of Sport* pp 1-29. Available online at http://journals.sagepub.com/doi/abs/10.1177/1012690216679835

Note on the contributors

Xavier Ramon-Vegas is a lecturer in the Department of Communication of Pompeu Fabra University. He holds a PhD in Communication from the UPF. He is also affiliated to the Olympic Studies Centre at the Autonomous University of Barcelona (CEO-UAB). His research focuses on media ethics and accountability and sports journalism. He has been a visiting researcher at the University of Stirling, the University of Glasgow, the University of Alabama and the IOC Olympic Studies Centre. Contact details: Xavier Ramon-Vegas, Pompeu Fabra University, Roc Boronat 138. 08018 Barcelona, Spain. Email: xavier.ramon@upf.edu

José-Luis Rojas-Torrijos is a lecturer in journalism at the University of Seville and EUSA Business University. He also participates in the MA programmes in journalism

Xavier Ramon-Vegas

José-Luis Rojas-Torrijos

and sports communication of the Pontifical University of Salamanca, Pompeu Fabra University, European University in Madrid, San Antonio Catholic University in Murcia and Marca-CEU University. He holds a PhD in Journalism (2010) and a BA in Information Sciences (1994) from the University of Seville. His research focuses on sports journalism, ethics and stylebooks. Contact details: José-Luis Rojas-Torrijos, University of Seville, Avda. Américo Vespucio, s/n. 41092 Sevilla, Spain. Email: jlrojas@us.es

Tom Bradshaw

Self-censorship and the pursuit of truth in sports journalism: A case study of David Walsh

Issues of self-censorship and potential barriers to truth-telling among sports journalists are explored through a case study of David Walsh, the award-winning Sunday Times *chief sports writer who is best known for his investigative work covering cycling. The paper uses a Kantian theoretical perspective to explore how sports journalists, including Walsh, implicitly use deontological and consequentialist modes of moral reasoning when making decisions about newsgathering and publication. Kant's categorical imperative is adapted as the* journalistic categorical imperative *which, together with the* journalistic hypothetical imperative, *is developed as a concept to explore the practical reasoning of sports journalists. Walsh's autobiographical writings about his sports reporting are analysed, together with the body of articles that he has written while a staff reporter at* The Sunday Times. *The case study aims to identify and highlight a range of ethical issues facing contemporary sports journalists, particularly self-censorship.*

Key words: self-censorship, sports journalism, David Walsh, Immanuel Kant, truth, categorical imperative

'Walsh is the worst journalist I know. There are journalists who are willing to lie, to threaten people and to steal in order to catch me out. All this for a sensational story. Ethics, standards, values, accuracy – these are of no interest to people like Walsh.'

Lance Armstrong, quoted in *De Telegraaf* (Walsh 2012: 260)

'David Walsh led a fight for the very soul of sport. This award is for a man who put his life on hold in search of a truth.'

Sir Matthew Pinsent, presenting the Barclays Lifetime Achievement Award to David Walsh at the 2013 BT Sport Industry Awards (*The Sunday Times*, Sport p. 4, 5 May 2013)

Tom Bradshaw

Introduction

This paper analyses the work of award-winning sports journalist David Walsh in order to identify and illuminate central ethical issues facing the contemporary sports journalist. Walsh is an Irish journalist based in the UK best known for his investigative reporting for *The Sunday Times* about the American cyclist Lance Armstrong, whom he suspected of taking performance-enhancing drugs (Fearon 2012). His 13-year investigation culminated in Armstrong being stripped of all seven of his Tour de France titles for doping, and Walsh receiving national awards for the quality of his journalism (Greenslade 2014; *The Sunday Times* 2012 and 2013). This case study also aims to function as what Yin refers to as an 'exploratory phase of an investigation' (Yin 2009: 6), enabling key ethical issues to emerge that can then be used to inform subsequent research into sports journalism ethics.

The study uses a Kantian theoretical perspective to identify and explore ethical concepts, tensions and incongruities arising in Walsh's published work, and as a prism from which to approach sports journalism ethics more generally. It is argued that Walsh's journalism and reflections on his practice contain a register that is strongly deontological, or duty-based, which contrasts with the more professionally pragmatic approach to journalistic practice that Walsh attributes to a number of colleagues. Kant's concepts of the hypothetical imperative and the categorical imperative, along with those of the autonomous moral agent and the heteronomous moral agent, are adapted and deployed as part of an analysis that seeks to make explicit a distinction in sports journalists' contrasting approaches to ethical issues around newsgathering. Boyle's contention that 'too many journalists and former sports people abdicate their responsibility to report honestly because they may upset important people or damage their own career trajectory' (Boyle 2006b) is used to inform the discussion, as does the concomitant question of the extent to which Walsh and other sports journalists self-censor. This develops work done by Binns (2017), whose primarily quantitative study found that self-censorship occurred not just among UK news journalists but among sports journalists too.

Literature review

This case study aims principally to explore the issue of self-censorship in sports journalism, a notion that research into sports journalism has hinted at without making explicit. In his monograph examining issues affecting modern sports journalism practice, Boyle contends that the closeness of the relationship between sports journalists and many of the teams that they cover means they run the risk of producing content that is 'complicit' with those organisations' aims (Boyle 2006a). Quoting the Irish sports journalist Tom Humphries, Boyle refers to this as the danger of 'travelling too close to the circus' and suggests a need for the sports media to 'run away from the circus' (Boyle 2006b). Rowe has suggested that sports journalists have performed a 'cheerleading' function rather than that of 'watchdog' (Rowe 2005 and 2007). The literature mainly focuses on the relationship between sports journalists and their sources: implicit within it is the argument that too close a relationship can lead to the journalist's self-imposed muffling of the truth – self-censorship.

Rowe, in considering whether there is substance to the claim that the sports desk is the 'toy department' of the newsroom, argues that a closeness of relationship between sports reporter and their subject is symptomatic of the one-dimensional, intellectually impoverished form of journalism that sports journalists provide. He accuses the sports media of:

> ... an excessively close integration with the sports industry, a lack of critical ambition, and an unimaginative reliance on socially and politically de-contextualized preview, description and retrospection regarding sporting events. When sources are used, they tend to be drawn from the ranks of celebrity athletes, coaches and administrators, thus further isolating the sports desk from the world beyond sport. The key question is, therefore, not whether sports journalism is, indeed, the toy department of the news media, but whether its controllers and practitioners are content to operate within the self-imposed and isolating limits that leave it continually open to professional challenge and even contempt (Rowe 2007: 400-401).

The allegation of 'self-imposed and isolating limits' is a significant one because it raises both ethical and epistemological questions about sports journalism. If sports journalists are, as Rowe suggests, complacently operating within a narrow world of their own creation, then the question arises over how the truth can be accessed and reported. Furthermore, if the nature of their working practices means they can not get to 'the truth', then it may be reasonably asked how sports journalists can fulfil the first criterion of almost every code of editorial practice, which is to report accurately.

Questions of self-censorship lurk in a number of writings about sports journalism but the phenomenon is rarely named. Andrews contends that 'sports journalists should always take care not to offend the sensibilities of others' (2014: 85) but gives no argument as to why sports journalists should tread so careful a line, while Boyle discusses one journalist, Eamon Dunphy's, refusal to tow what Dunphy terms the 'soft consensus'. Boyle adds: 'Too many journalists and former sports people abdicate their responsibility to report honestly because they may upset important people or damage their own career trajectory' (Boyle 2006b). Similarly, in an analysis of whether former retired athletes make good sports

Tom Bradshaw

journalists, a former *BBC Sport* editor suggests that the introduction of ex-professionals into the media is actually fostering a culture of self-censorship, with former players talking in platitudes for fear of upsetting clubs with whom they have had a professional connection (Bose 2012).

Allegations of sports journalists self-censoring to the detriment of truth have been made from within the industry as well as from without. A former national tabloid editor, who has himself had a questionable relationship with the truth at certain moments in his career (MacKenzie 2016), alleged in a *Sun* column that 'the real bad boys' during Sam Allardyce's removal as England manager in 2016 following a *Daily Telegraph* exposé of questionable behaviour that compromised the coach's position were sports journalists. Under the headline 'Sports mafia that's kept Big Sam's secrets safe for years', MacKenzie effectively re-asserted Boyle's claims of journalistic complicity with the sports stars they are covering, and claimed that too many sports journalists put the enhancement of their own career trajectory ahead of telling the truth and exposing corruption.

David Walsh, the subject of this case study, has principally covered cycling during his career and Sefiha's (2010) ethnographic study of a US cycling magazine's coverage of the use of performance-enhancing drugs (PEDs) is pertinent. The study considers issues of self-censorship without explicitly using the term, instead referring in one instance to reporters 'exercising discretion' (Sefiha 2010: 209). The extent to which exposing PED use can 'severely compromise' (ibid) relationships with sources is discussed, and it is suggested that this can cause hesitancy among journalists in publishing the truth. Sefiha highlights the professional dilemma that confronts sports journalists – specifically cycling journalists – in this context: either expose wrongdoing and be ousted from the inner circle so that one can no longer report on the sport effectively on a daily basis from the 'inside'; or keep quiet about the wrongdoing so that one preserves source relations and is able to report effectively – that is, with access to sources – from the inside on a day-by-day basis (ibid).

While not invoking the consequentialist-deontological dichotomy of moral philosophy that informs this paper, Sefiha indicates that many journalists on the magazine he studied took a consequentialist approach to their fact selection, while simultaneously speaking in the deontological language of obligations and duties. This consequentialist-deontological tension is illustrated by the use of competing phrases such as 'foreseeing the results' of an action on the one hand and talk of 'an obligation, regardless of its effects' on the other (ibid: 209-210). Sefiha's study, therefore, helps inform a useful methodological lens with which to approach this study.

Methodology

This case study takes as its unit of analysis David Walsh's journalism, and the two primary data sets are the articles he wrote at *The Sunday Times* up to November 2017, and the books he has published while working for that title. It also considers a range of other data, including broadcast interviews that Walsh has given and reviews of his books.

Why David Walsh?

The quotations about Walsh that preface this paper contain abstract nouns which denote values that are central to debates around sports journalism ethics and wider journalistic practice: truth, standards, accuracy. Walsh has stated that while working on the Armstrong investigation, he knew it would be the story that would 'define' him as a journalist (*The Sunday Times*, Sport p. 4, 5 May 2013; BBC 2017), and it was during his coverage of this story that the ethical dimension of his work became most apparent, as the quotations above from Armstrong (in Walsh, 2012: 260) and the citation for an award read by Pinsent (*The Sunday Times*, May 2013) underscore.

Before deciding on David Walsh as the subject for this case study, the researcher supplemented his pre-existing awareness of Walsh's work with a wider reading of his output and others' reflections on it. It was during this review that his suitability as the subject of a study was established. While lionised in some quarters as an exemplar of the intrepid investigative sports journalist who is unafraid to speak truth to power and hold powerful governing bodies to account (Greenslade 2014), an initial reading of Walsh's autobiographical works as well as the wider secondary literature about his sports journalism revealed a more nuanced and complex picture.

As has been seen in the literature review, a recurring, negative description of sports journalism in the academic literature is that of it being the 'toy department' of the newsroom, with sports journalists too often fulfilling a 'cheerleading' function of the sports they cover (Rowe 2005, 2007) and Walsh – at various stages of his career – has had claims of cheerleading made against him (McKay 2010; BBC 2017). Turning the spotlight on himself, he too has admitted that at certain times in his career he has fulfilled that role, even suppressing certain stories (Walsh 2012) through a process that could be characterised as self-censorship. The analysis and discussion section below highlights how these periods of 'cheerleading' – acknowledged or alleged – occurred either side of Walsh's coverage of the Armstrong case, making the ethical trajectory of his career, therefore, a complex one. It was this element of apparent incongruity that reinforced the initial hunch that he would be an illuminating subject for an exploratory case study.

PAPER

Tom Bradshaw   *A Kantian theoretical perspective*
This case study's exploration of Walsh's output and journalistic approach is analysed through the perspective of Kantian practical reasoning (Kant 1997 [1788], 2005 [1785]). In his writings on ethics and the formulation of his categorical imperative, Immanuel Kant (1724-1804) invokes the distinction between decisions that are taken as a means of accomplishing something else (instrumental reasoning based on 'hypothetical imperatives') and decisions that are made because the action underpinned by that decision represents an action that is of value in itself. The latter type of reasoning, which manifests itself in the edicts of duty, admits of no exceptions (it is universal and categorical) and the moral agent is obligated to do it (it is imperative). Taking Walsh's writings and career as its focus, this paper uses a Kantian idiom to analyse the ethical and practical decisions that sports journalists make in the course of gathering and publishing their stories.

In particular, this paper focuses on the tension that arises in Walsh's writings – and in his own deliberations on other journalists' actions – between what shall be termed the *journalistic hypothetical imperative* to maintain access, contacts and, thereby, the flow of stories, and the *journalistic categorical imperative* to pursue and report the truth regardless of the professional consequences. Through a consideration of this dichotomy, this paper explores the fissure that exists in sports journalism between those whose professional practice is driven by instrumental reasoning and those who adopt a deontological approach. The former are motivated by the aim – or need – to maintain access and contacts for the sake of then being able to fulfil certain journalistic goals (e.g. meeting a deadline, meeting a story quota, satisfying an editor), while the latter place certain duties at the heart of sports journalism and declare, implicitly or explicitly, that those values are inviolable. While this distinction would appear to split journalists firmly into two groups, there is blurring and overlap, with some journalists – at different times in their careers, or even at different times covering the same story – moving from one position of practical reasoning into the other, a phenomenon indicated by Sefiha (2010).

The hypothetical imperative takes the structure of an 'If ..., then...' (e. g. 'If you want to retain good interview access to players at a Premier League club, then agree to the club's request to have the opportunity to approve copy before it is published'). In such instances, the imperative states the means to achieving the hypothetical end. Kant suggests that such hypothetical imperatives are always conditional, in that they provide a reason only for the person who desires the end stated in the first part of the imperative and impose no obligation on anyone whose desires are different to it.

The categorical imperative, by contrast, is a form of imperative that is unconditional. Rather than involving the currency of conditional 'ifs', the categorical imperative deals in the currency of unconditional 'oughts' (e. g. the categorical speaks in terms of inviolable principles such as 'You ought to tell the truth' and 'You ought to try to expose wrongdoing'). When deliberating on what the end of my action ought to be, the categorical imperative states that I, as a moral agent, am constrained by reason to 'act only on that maxim which I can at the same time will as a universal law' (Kant 2005 [1785]). So, the Kantian journalist could argue that publishing an article that withheld the truth, or deliberately not pursuing a story despite having some evidence or hunch of wrongdoing, is morally wrong because such decisions, if applied universally (made a 'universal law'), would lead to contradiction and the collapse of journalistic communication; in other words, they have an illogicality to them that reason resists.

There is another distinction that Kant draws which will be used in this paper as a tool to analyse Walsh's output and career. This is the distinction between the 'autonomous' moral agent – the person who behaves according to the dictates of their independent reason and will – and the 'heteronomous' person whose will is constrained by external forces, such as their individual desires or the aim of satisfying the wishes of an outside authority, such as a parent or a perceived god-like figure (ibid).

The autonomy/heteronomy distinction in this case study is used to try to illuminate the different mindsets required by sports journalists when covering ethically contentious stories. Journalism is a deadline-driven industry and, in the digital age, the need to hit website story quotas and visitors is paramount. The pressure to meet these deadlines and quotas is passed down from an editor, and it could be argued that a reporter who works in these circumstances and feels their pressure – and who adapts their behaviour accordingly – works *heteronomously*. Such a reporter is likely to feel the pull of the journalistic hypothetical imperative described above.

Analysis and discussion
David Walsh the Kantian
There are passages in his writings where Walsh displays a distinctly Kantian moral stance. For instance, Walsh contends that any attempt to produce sports journalism that does not comply with the imperative of honestly pursuing the truth, regardless of professional cost, is illogical and contradictory. This position is conveyed by Walsh in both his own account of his pursuit of Lance Armstrong (Walsh 2012), and also in an interview given to the BBC's *HARDtalk* programme: 'As a journalist you're thinking, if this is the greatest fraud, and you believe it's the greatest fraud, you have an absolute responsibility to go after it and reveal him to be a fraud' (BBC 2017:

Tom Bradshaw

3.42-3.51). The key term here is 'absolute responsibility'; the sports journalist's unconditional duty is to attempt to expose the truth. It is, for Walsh, a journalistic categorical imperative. In another interview, Walsh expresses it another way by saying he would have felt 'a fake' if he had scaled back his investigation of Armstrong for fear of jeopardising interview access (Bailey 2015).

There are also passages in *Seven deadly sins* (his account of the Armstrong investigation) where Walsh vigorously asserts a form of what could be categorised as Kantian autonomy. He recounts how he dissented from the positions adopted by *The Sunday Times*' sports desk and the newspaper's lawyer over what the newspaper should publish about the cyclist amid their fears of the paper being sued for libel (Walsh 2012). This disagreement, and Walsh's reluctance to have his work diluted, reached the point of Walsh tendering his resignation. In this, Walsh displays his resistance to heteronomy; his moral will is his, and his sense of duty trumps the moral force of claims made upon him from without by others, including senior colleagues at his employer. However, it is too simple to state that Walsh is a straightforward Kantian and that his entire corpus is underpinned by a deontological morality.

Going with the tide versus resisting the tide
Going with the tide and resisting the tide is a metaphor that recurs in Walsh's writings and public pronouncements about his work covering Armstrong. For Walsh, being prepared to resist the currents that provide an easy swim through one's career is vital, for without such resistance the sports journalist is open to being swept along on the surface, without investigating the eddies deeper down. When Walsh first met and interviewed Armstrong in 1993, the 21-year-old cyclist's personality is described as being 'like a wave crashing forward and carrying you with him … he had me at his side, and on his side' (Walsh 2012: 2). But resisting the pull of the wave is important, as Walsh described when delivering the 2014 Hugh Cudlipp Lecture. 'A good story is always worth pursuing,' he said, and for the sake of the pursuit 'it's OK to swim against the tide' (Greenslade 2014).

Walsh is frank in acknowledging the sense of warm feeling and goodwill that can exist between a journalist and those they are covering; a feeling that can verge on hero-worship. 'The man-crush is a hazard of life for the sportswriter' (Walsh 2012: 2), he writes, referring both to his initial meeting with Armstrong and his work a decade earlier covering the Irish cyclist Sean Kelly. Reading Walsh's account of that time covering Kelly, a number of themes emerge: of confessed self-censorship; of Walsh literally riding too close to the circus; and of the blurring power of the sports man-crush. When, in 1982, Walsh covered his first Tour de France, he describes how he travelled with Kelly's fiancée and her father – so, to continue Boyle's metaphor (2006b), right at the centre of the circus. And then, two years later during a Paris to Brussels race, while writing a biography of Kelly, Walsh – while not using the term – produced what, in light of the Armstrong investigation, now appears a dissonant piece of self-censorship that resulted in the public being denied knowledge of Kelly's drug-taking. Inherent in Walsh's account, which merits being stated at some length, is a sense of complicity in a story being swept under the carpet, and a retrospective sense of the absence of integrity and professionalism.

> It was time for Kelly to get himself to the start line. He stood up, hopped on his bike. … As he did there was the unmistakable sound of pills rattling inside a small plastic container. … It should have been a seminal moment. We had inadvertently seen the realities of professional cycling, but we weren't ready for that. I had a biography to write, one in which the hero is a farmer's son from Carrick-on-Suir, a man who as a boy had eaten raw turnips when hungry. … Pills rattling against plastic didn't fit the story. When you're a fan, as I was, you don't ask the hero about the sound that came from his pocket (Walsh 2012: 16-17).

At the end of the day's racing, Kelly tested positive for the banned drug Stimul and was later fined 1,000 Swiss francs and given a one-month suspended sentence. Walsh continued:

> When I wrote about the 1984 Paris-Brussels in the biography, I didn't mention the pills in the morning and I tried to make the case that it was hard to believe Kelly had used a substance so easily detectable. I chose to see the ridiculous leniency of the authorities as proof that, at worst, it was a minor infraction. It wasn't how a proper journalist would have reacted. At the time I knew what I was doing (Walsh 2012: 16-18).

In this instance, Walsh self-censored – he prevented the truth from being published and disseminated – and in so doing he produced an instance of the *journalistic hypothetical imperative* mentioned above: that in order to maintain his access and friendship to professional cyclist Sean Kelly, Walsh sidelined values and put pragmatism in their place. This, writes Walsh, was not the behaviour of 'a proper journalist', implying that an authentic journalist would not conceal facts for pragmatic or emotional reasons but would, instead, behave with more integrity. Self-censorship, therefore, emerges as a concept right at the centre of a study into the ethics of sports journalism.

The notion of what a 'proper' journalist should do is one that infuses *Seven deadly sins*. Walsh believes that the adage of holding the powerful to account applies equally to sport as it does to news reporting:

Tom Bradshaw
Some of the more thoughtful practitioners of our trade like to say that if you are to be a sportswriter it's better to love the writing more than the sport. I loved the sport. I loved the role that sportswriters could play in sport: afflicting the comfortable, comforting the afflicted, as news reporters used to say. No longer did I see it as our role to smile up at the dais for a press conference, reassuring the organisers and competitors that 'there aren't nobody here but us chickens'. ... I didn't want to be a fool just because of my love for sport. And I didn't want to act as an agent in making fools of readers and fans on behalf of the UCI [Union Cycliste Internationale] (2012: 70-71).

In places, Walsh's contempt for those colleagues whom he believes are complicit in 'making fools of readers and fans' is vividly expressed. Faced with a choice between nurturing contacts through the avoidance of posing awkward questions, or jeopardising that access by holding the powerful to account, Walsh's position is clear, and he provides that clarity by means of contrast. The contrast is with John Wilcockson, a journalist for *Velo News* with whom Walsh shared a car on the 1999 Tour. Walsh describes Wilcockson as being on something akin to a professional life-support machine, with the oxygen for his career being supplied by the quotations provided by access to leading athletes:

> He couldn't live on this race without access to certain riders; namely the top Americans and Lance. He would do the bread-and-butter job of reporting better the most, but for him the cream came in the team hotel in the evening, when you might snatch a fifteen- or twenty-minute interview with one of your favourites (Walsh 2012: 69).

Here, Walsh the unflinching deontologist is most clearly in evidence. He refuses to 'act as an agent in making fools of readers' but, instead, determinedly pursues a line of investigation that derives entirely from his own mission to get to the truth – his is the journalism of autonomy. That autonomy will not be surrendered for the sake of gaining smoother access to athletes or teams. Duty to pursue the underlying truth is placed before professional pragmatism, while for Wilcockson it is the other way around: the need to gain quotes means the need to gain access which means the requirement not to ask difficult questions, even if those are the questions that might lead to the truth.

Walsh's disdain for elements within the media is powerfully conveyed in his recollections of covering the 1999 Tour. The press tent, he writes, is 'crammed to dangerous levels with sycophants and time servers', while journalists are part of the 'confederacy of cheerleaders' who protect Armstrong, along with administrators at the sport's governing body, the Union Cycliste Internationale (2012: 88).

An important concept that can be derived from Walsh's reflections on his professional practice is the self-censorship of *questions* as well as the self-censorship of published *statements*. If a journalist censors the type of question he poses, then he is indirectly muzzling the output, too. With Armstrong's 1999 Tour victory, Walsh suggests that journalists self-censored their line of questioning (although he does not use that idiom) out of a misplaced respect for the fact that Armstrong had only overcome testicular cancer two years later. 'I think part of the reason they didn't want to ask those questions was because the guy had come back from cancer. For me, that was irrelevant. I just didn't think that should stop us from asking questions' (Pugh 2012).

Embedded sports journalism – Inside Team Sky

A key issue in Walsh's career, however, is how compatible his disdain for the 'confederacy of cheerleaders' is with him accepting an offer to be embedded with a cycling team; and a cycling team with a stated agenda to portray itself as clean. This is a tension at the heart of Walsh's work, given Walsh's acceptance of an offer to live and travel with Team Sky in 2013.

PAPER

Both at the time of accepting the invitation from Team Sky's Dave Brailsford and since the publication of his subsequent book, *Inside Team Sky*, Walsh has been accused of opening himself up to claims of 'cheerleading' (BBC 2017). The issue can also be expressed in terms of whether in this instance Walsh pursued professional pragmatism – the *journalism hypothetical imperative* – at the expense of detached, journalistic activity that would have enabled the *journalism categorical imperative* of pursuing and publishing the truth to be fulfilled. Moreover, to continue the Kantian idiom, by accepting the opportunity to be 'embedded' Walsh was surrendering his autonomy and, instead, allowing heteronomous factors to influence his journalism and newsgathering methods. The claim of cheerleading arguably gained greater power when allegations of improper use by Team Sky of the Therapeutic Use Exemption (TUE) process involving performance-enhancing drugs subsequently emerged, with the claims focused on former lead cyclist Bradley Wiggins. BBC interviewer Stephen Sackur challenged Walsh over this in a vivid manner:

> Why oh why, having learned the lessons you did from the Armstrong case, did you decide in more recent years to vouch for in a really significant way the honesty, the integrity, the credibility of the dominant cycling team of recent years, Team Sky, when so many other journalists were saying: 'Hang on a minute, you can't be so sure that they're clean when cycling as a whole is still full of drugs' – why did you do that? (BBC 2017: 10:44-11:12).

Tom Bradshaw   Critically, in the same interview, Walsh went on to state that – in light of subsequent facts that had emerged over Wiggins' use of TUEs – he felt he had been 'duped' by Brailsford. What is surprising here is arguably not the allegation itself but the fact that the award-winning, ethically-driven journalist who helped bring Lance Armstrong to account is acknowledging that he had allowed himself to be compromised.

Walsh's decision-making around the *Inside Team Sky* project raises a number of ethical issues. One is around whether embedding of this nature is ever ethically justifiable by a sports journalist, or whether it inherently runs the risk of being tantamount to – or close to – cheerleading or unwitting collusion. The second, more general area is around the long-standing question about the distance that should ideally exist between sports journalists and the subjects of their reporting. Both in the book and subsequently, Walsh has argued that his time with Team Sky did not involve him breaking his ethical principles, while also conceding – as the 'dupe' allegation suggests – that he was to an extent manipulated.

There is evidence that Walsh's time with Team Sky did not prompt him to go 'soft' on the team and its cyclists. The year after he had been embedded with Sky, Walsh published a questioning piece about the use of an asthma-reliever by top Team Sky cyclist Chris Froome during the Tour of Romandie (Walsh, *The Sunday Times*, Sport p. 18, 22 June 2014). And earlier that month, he also wrote an opinion piece focusing on the tense relationship between Froome and Bradley Wiggins (Walsh, *The Sunday Times*, Sport p. 18, 8 June 2014). In a piece reflecting on Wiggins' retirement, Walsh uses strong terms when describing Wiggins' 2012 Tour de France victory. 'That victory is tainted, diminished, and when you're done wrestling with the issues thrown up by his team's application for therapeutic use exemptions on his behalf, you just want to throw the 2012 Tour de France victory into the bin and wish it had never happened' (Walsh, *The Sunday Times*, Sport, 1 January 2017 p. 16).

Walsh states with some confidence in *Inside Team Sky* that his spell within the team was a fact-finding assignment that generated conclusions reached through *bona fide* journalism. He states:

> In the house of Team Sky I have looked around. I have asked the questions. Done the journalism I came to do. Nobody has given me a secret handshake or password signifying membership of the Masonic Lodge of Supreme Wizard Murdoch. Nobody has slammed doors in my face. And I have concluded that Chris Froome exists within Team Sky because he is an almost unstoppable force, one of those freak talents which, against all odds, somehow bubbles to the top (2013: 193).

Walsh's decision to accept an invitation to spend time with Team Sky is arguably a case study in its own right about sports journalism ethics, not least given the latest allegations surrounding Froome and asthma medication (Ingle and Kelner 2017). It has highlighted how the Kantian journalistic duty to pursue and publish the truth is potentially incompatible with the embedding process, despite there being scope for acknowledging that the integrity of Walsh's work was not totally undermined by the embedding. The independence – or autonomy – of sports journalists is a key area posed by Walsh's embedding, with the issue of how best to access 'the truth' another central topic.

Conclusion

This case study of David Walsh has highlighted a number of key areas for further research in the field of sports journalism ethics. Principally, it has highlighted how issues of self-censorship are central to the ethics of sports journalism and how the integrity of the profession can arguably be measured by the extent to which its practitioners self-censor, whether that be through the self-censoring of *questions* or the self-censoring of *information* that is contained in published material. Walsh's own career has also been shown to be an instructive one to analyse from the perspective of deontology, with his work shifting between an apparently firm adherence to a duty-based approach to an instance of him potentially surrendering professional autonomy.

PAPER

References

Andrews, P. (2014) *Sports journalism: A practical introduction*, London, Sage, second edition

Bailey, M. (2015) David Walsh on Armstrong, Froome and making a movie, *cyclist. co.uk*, 28 October. Available online at http://www.cyclist.co.uk/news/551/david-walsh-on-armstrong-froome-and-making-a-movie, accessed on 20 July 2017

BBC (2017) *HARDtalk*, 20 February. Available online as a podcast at http://www.bbc.co.uk/programmes/p04sqp3n, accessed on 11 August 2017

Binns, A. (2017a) 'Fair game? Journalists' experiences of online abuse', *Applied Journal of Journalism and Media Studies*, Vol. 6, No. 2 pp 183-206

Boyle, R. (2006a) *Sports journalism: Context and issues*, London, Sage

Boyle, R. (2006b) Running away from the circus, *British Journalism Review*, Vol. 17, No. 3 pp 12-17. Available online at http://www.bjr.org.uk/data/2006/no3_boyle, accessed on 28 November 2015

Bose, M. (2012) But can medalists write?, *British Journalism Review*, Vol. 23, No. 4 pp 8-11. Available online at http://www.bjr.org.uk/data/2012/no4_bose, accessed on 28 November 2015

Fearon, M. (2012) In pursuit of the truth, *The Sunday Times*, Culture 16 December p. 41

Greenslade, R. (2014) How I brought down drug-taking Lance Armstrong, by David Walsh, *Guardian*, 28 January. Available online at https://www.theguardian.com/media/greenslade/2014/jan/28/lance-armstrong-sundaytimes., accessed on 21 June 2017

Tom Bradshaw

Ingle, S. and Kelner, M. (2017) Chris Froome fights to save career after failed drugs test result, *Guardian*, 13 December. Available online at https://www.theguardian.com/sport/2017/dec/13/chris-froome-team-sky-reputation-abnormal-drug-test, accessed on 21 December 2017

Kant, I (1997 [1788]) *Critique of practical reason* (trans. by Abbott, T. K.), Cambridge, Cambridge University Press

Kant, I. (2005 [1785]) *The moral law: Groundwork of the metaphysic of morals* (trans. by Paton, H. J.), London, Taylor & Francis ebook

McKay, F. (2010) On doping and David Walsh, *podiumcafe.com*, 10 November. Available online at https://www.podiumcafe.com/2010/11/10/1805511/on-doping-and-david-walsh, accessed on 19 July 2017

MacKenzie, K. (2016) The sports mafia that's kept Big Sam's secrets safe for years, *thesun.co.uk*, 29 September. Available online at https://www.thesun.co.uk/news/1882085/the-sports-mafia-thats-kept-big-sams-secrets-safe-for-years/, accessed on 29 December 2017

Pugh, A. (2012) David Walsh: 'It was obvious to me Lance Armstrong was doping', *pressgazette.co.uk*, 11 October. Available online at http://www.pressgazette.co.uk/david-walsh-it-was-obvious-me-lance-armstrong-was-doping/, accessed on 20 July 2017

Rowe, D. (2005) Fourth estate or fan club? Sports journalism engages the popular, Allan, S. (ed.) *Journalism: Critical issues*, Maidenhead, Open University Press pp 125-136

Rowe, D. (2007) Sports journalism: Still the 'toy department' of the news media?, *Journalism*, Vol. 8, No. 4 pp 384-405

Sefiha, O. (2010) Now's when we throw him under the bus: Institutional and occupational identities and the coverage of doping in sport, *Sociology of Sport Journal*, Vol. 27 pp 200-218

Walsh, D. (2012) *The program: Seven deadly sins – My pursuit of Lance Armstrong*, London, Simon & Schuster

Walsh, D. (2013) *Inside Team Sky*, London, Simon & Schuster

Yin, R. K. (2009) *Case study research: Design and methods*, London, Sage, fourth edition

The Sunday Times (2012) David Walsh scoops Journalist of the Year Award, Sport, 9 December p. 15

The Sunday Times (2013) David Walsh honoured over 13-year fight 'for the very soul of sport'. Sport, 5 May p. 4

Note on the contributor

Tom Bradshaw is course leader and senior lecturer in Sports Journalism at the University of Gloucestershire. He studied philosophy at Cambridge University before becoming a journalist and has won awards for his sports journalism. He is midway through a PhD that examines ethical issues in contemporary sports journalism.

Simon McEnnis

A comparative analysis of how regulatory codes inform broadcast and print sports journalists' work routines in the UK using *Sky Sports News* and the *Sun* as case studies

This paper aims to provide a comparative analysis of how regulatory codes influence the work routines of print and broadcast sports journalists in the UK. Sky Sports News *24-hour news channel and the* Sun *newspaper are used as case studies. The government-regulated broadcast industry interprets autonomy as independence from advertisers and sponsors. Regulation, therefore, creates challenges for broadcast journalists within a hyper-commercialised professional sports environment. Conversely, the press regulator, the Independent Press Standards Organisation (IPSO) focuses on autonomy from government rather than business. Print sports journalists, therefore, lack autonomy from commercial pressures as media managers can exercise a degree of editorial control. This analysis examines sports journalism's fragmented professional culture while arguing that broadcast sports journalists' ethical conduct is more complex than has previously been acknowledged.*

Key words: sports journalism, regulation, the *Sun*, *Sky Sports News*, ethics

Introduction

Occupational studies on UK sports journalists have overlooked the role that regulation plays in work routines and experiences (Rowe 2004, Boyle 2006). This study defines the professional group as consisting of both broadcast and print sports journalists as a broader community of practice (Boyle and Hutchins 2017). However, print and broadcast sports journalists are governed by different regulatory codes. Print sports journalists working for national newspapers follow a self-regulatory model through the Independent Press Standards Organisation (IPSO) editors' code of

Simon McEnnis

practice. Broadcast sports journalists are regulated by the Office of Communications (Ofcom) broadcasting code.

Regulation and ethics have been prominent topics in contemporary UK media debates – particularly since the *News of the World*, a weekly Sunday tabloid newspaper, was exposed in 2011 to be hacking mobile phone voicemails as a story-gathering practice. The government held a judicial public inquiry (chaired by Lord Justice Brian Leveson) into the practices and ethics of the press during 2011 and 2012 and this led to recommendations that the UK press be regulated by an independent organisation backed by a royal charter. Regulation continues to dominate industry debates. The government has created an independent regulator, Impress, but most of the national media have refused to recognise it, preferring, instead, to maintain the self-regulatory system through IPSO.

This study explores the key distinctions between these two regulatory codes before analysing how their provisions apply to both the print and broadcast contexts. This analysis was conducted using Deuze's conceptual tool of occupational ideology. Deuze (2005) notes that journalists' professional principles can be defined as objectivity, autonomy, ethics, immediacy and public service. We can, therefore, expect regulatory codes to reflect these core journalistic principles. The study aims to provide an enhanced understanding of sports journalists' professional culture, specifically the commonalities and differences across the traditional platforms of television and print. Recent research into sports journalists has tended to focus on the transition from analogue to digital platforms (Sherwood and Nicholson 2012, McEnnis 2013, McGuire and Murray 2013, 2016). However, this paper argues that there is still 'unfinished business' in the exploration of occupational routines in more traditional settings.

This study is also informed by the researcher's reflections on his involvement in both print and broadcast sports journalism: specifically as:

- a sports journalist with the *Sun* between 2000 and 2009 before moving into academia. The author also worked 'overtime' shifts with the *Sun*'s sister paper at News International (now News UK), the *News of the World*, from 2000 until its closure in 2011 and

- the leader of an advanced sports journalism staff development programme with *Sky Sports News* from 2011 to the present. A particular programme, delivered by the author to 20 broadcast sports journalists between February and July 2017, ran across 19 three-hour weekly sessions and was accredited by the National Council for the Training of Journalists (NCTJ). The sessions were discussion-based with the author's reflections on these conversations informing this study. Candidates on the course granted their written consent for these discussions to be used for research purposes.

The *Sun* is regulated by IPSO while *Sky Sports News* falls under Ofcom's remit. Both news organisations are part of the Rupert Murdoch media empire (as was the *News of the World* before its closure) and are stylistically alike in their sports news presentation with similar target audiences of predominantly younger males. The *Sun* and *Sky Sports News* are mainly interested in celebrity sports stories and sports events. Transfer gossip, breaking news and soft interviews with sports people are key features. Both aim to break exclusive sports news stories. Therefore, journalists at both organisations share similar outlooks to work practices and daily routines.

Previous research has found that that sports journalists adopt low ethical standards (Rowe 2004, Sugden and Tomlinson 2007). Sports journalists are considered to be too close to sources to the extent that their loyalties lie with protecting and insulating contacts rather than serving the public. Collusive practices with other reporters are common (Sugden and Tomlinson 2007). However, the issue of regulation is largely absent from these analyses. For instance, Raymond Boyle's (2006) otherwise excellent occupational study of UK sports journalists glosses over how regulation informs their routines and practices.

A comparison of Ofcom and IPSO regulatory codes
Until recently, the BBC was regulated by its own Trust while commercial broadcasters were regulated by Ofcom. However, Ofcom became the first external regulator of the BBC in April 2017 (White 2017). The IPSO editors' code of practice governs most of the national news media although the *Guardian*, *Independent* and the *Financial Times* prefer their own internal complaints systems. The 23rd and most recent edition of the journalists' law 'bible', *McNae's essential law for journalists*, provides a useful industry justification for why two different codes of ethics govern UK media:

> The emotional impact of moving images and sounds, particularly on children in the audience, can be greater than that of printed text and still pictures – for example, if a programme has sexual content or shows death or violence. Also, the ability of television and radio to air material instantaneously means they have great potential to provoke immediate public disorder or violence (Hanna and Dodd 2016: 23-24).

Broadcast journalists, therefore, must conform to higher and more exacting ethical standards than their newspaper counterparts because of the power of the medium. Broadcast journalists also

Simon McEnnis

face more punitive measures than print should they infringe their regulatory code. Ofcom has a remit to withdraw broadcast licences and impose fines for the most serious offences For instance, in 2008, Independent Television (ITV) was fined £5.675m. for its misuse of premium rate phone lines (Conlan 2008). In practice, Ofcom rarely fines or removes licences and such severe punishments are reserved for the most serious infringements. Upheld complaints tend to result in warnings to broadcasters to improve their practices and procedures. IPSO, which is funded by the newspaper industry, can impose fines of up to £1m. unlike its forerunner, the Press Complaints Commission (PCC). However, there are doubts over whether IPSO plans to use these relatively new powers or if their introduction is merely an attempt to appease critics who accuse the regulator of being the PCC mark 2 (Harcup 2015).

The IPSO editors' code of practice and the Ofcom broadcasting code both contain similar interpretations of public interest that is based around exposing crime, breaches to public health and safety, incompetence affecting the public and misleading claims. The codes also aim to promote journalistic objectivity. IPSO's editors' code of practice states that journalists 'must distinguish between conjecture, comment and fact' while the Ofcom code contains an entire provision relating to impartiality. Both codes contain similar provisions on privacy, accuracy, harassment, children, discrimination and deception.

The key point of departure between the codes is the inclusion of commercial references in television programming as a provision (section 9) within the Ofcom broadcasting code. However, there is no mention of the need for newspaper journalists to be free of commercial influence on editorial decision-making. This provision essentially results from the differing interpretations of autonomy and independence within print and broadcast industries. The IPSO editors' code of practice considers autonomy in terms of independence from government involvement. Newspaper organisations' principal concern is to maintain its self-regulatory system, which they consider to be threatened by the outcome of the Leveson Inquiry and the emergence of an alternative, state-backed press regulator, Impress.

Newspaper journalists' sense of autonomy is tied to the notion of press freedom from state interference rather than commercial influences. Newspaper journalists do not see it as unethical that editorial policies are heavily influenced by the business and political agendas of newspaper owners. Indeed, journalistic objectivity and professionalism involve reporters being able to separate their own political views from the agendas of newspaper owners (Aldridge and Evetts 2003). In contrast, the broadcast industry, because it has been traditionally regulated by state-appointed bodies, interprets its autonomy as safeguarding editorial control from the influence of sponsors and advertisers.

Broadcast journalists are expected to exhibit greater awareness of the ethical implications of allowing 'unduly prominent' commercial references into television programming. Undue prominence means that a brand, product or service is particularly prevalent in the editorial content either visually or verbally. In this respect, the Ofcom broadcasting code speaks directly to the claim that the power of television creates a need for greater ethical responsibility. Ofcom states that the ethical implications of commercial references include loss of editorial control and independence from programming, blurring the distinction between editorial content and advertising, and failure to protect audiences from surreptitious advertising, financial harm or unsuitable sponsorship.

Print sports journalists and regulation

The role of newspaper sports journalists in the construction of important cultural meanings around sport has been highlighted by Boyle, Rowe and Whannel (2009). Moreover, the print tradition – built on the writings of such 'greats' as Neville Cardus (1888-1975), Frank Keating (1937-2013) and Ian Wooldridge (1932-2007), is reinforced and celebrated in award ceremonies such as that organised each year by the Sport Journalists' Association (McEnnis 2018).

The 'light touch' approach of press self-regulation compared to the 'heavier' approach of Ofcom is reflected in the work experiences of print sports journalists. My career as a sports journalist at the *Sun* newspaper occurred at a time when IPSO's forerunner, the PCC, existed. IPSO largely adopted the PCC's code of practice so there has been no substantive difference in the regulatory framework adhered to by print sports journalists since I left the industry in 2011. Further, a general resistance to regulation is embedded in the professional culture and the notion of 'means to an end' results in journalists preferring to be their own judges of whether any practice can be judged ethical or not (Aldridge and Evetts 2003). The *Sun* sports desk was not unduly concerned with separating facts from comment. Instead, the sports desk tended to perceive differing forms and styles as providing this distinction. For instance, the newspaper page was a place where you could clearly recognise more factually-driven news stories as different from more opinion-oriented column pieces.

Professional sports are highly commercialised. Public relations managers regularly attempt to interfere in the editorial decision-making process to ensure positive publicity and to protect image. The sports desk did sometimes allow media managers to be involved with the editorial process as the only way to secure

Simon McEnnis

relevant and interesting content, such as exclusive interviews with high-profile sports stars. And there was nothing in the regulatory code of practice that could act as a deterrent in this respect.

Big exclusive interviews with celebrity footballers, for instance, were often subjected to 'copy approval' by either club PR departments, sponsors or management companies. Copy approval involved having a story vetted by a newsroom outsider and this ceding of editorial autonomy and control is ethically problematic. Sports desks have historically focused their coverage almost exclusively on professional sport, particularly the most financially lucrative (Boyle and Haynes 2009). Copy approval can be seen as an evolution of that relationship. There are three key reasons why this situation has arisen.

- Firstly, newspapers have little economic power within the professional sports environment which is defined by multi-billion-pound TV deals for screening live sport. As a result, sports journalists must carefully negotiate their access to high-profile sports people and the nature of these arrangements will often be conditional on publicising a particular brand, product, service or even charitable foundation.

- Secondly, external agencies such as club PR departments, sponsors and advertisers recognise the advantages that a message appearing in a newspaper product can provide compared to their own internally-produced messages such as websites, matchday programmes and advertisements.

- Thirdly, the fact that IPSO does not mention corporate or commercial conflicts in its regulatory code not only means that there is no deterrent but that copy approval is a legitimate route in securing sought-after and highly-prized sports content.

Broadcast sports journalism and regulation
Research to date has tended to concentrate on sports reporters in newspapers (Boyle 2006, Hutchins and Rowe 2012, McEnnis 2013, 2015, 2016). As a result, little is known about broadcast sports journalists. Previous research into sports broadcasting also tends to focus on commentators and presenters rather than reporters (Whannel 1992, Rowe 2004). Broadcast sports journalism is often discussed from the perspectives of print sports journalists, who express concern that rolling 24-hour news channels are dumbing down professional standards (Sugden and Tomlinson 2010).

Sky Sports News has been a driving force in the growth of broadcast sports journalism in the UK. The 24-hour rolling news channel was launched in 1998 after *Sky Sports* managing director Vic Wakeling came across the idea while watching the business channel, Bloomberg (Kelner 2013). *Sky Sports News* is only available to watch with a pay-TV subscription and promotes televised live sport screened on sister *Sky Sports* channels. However, *Sky Sports News* journalists are recognisably 'journalistic' in their professional practice. Reporters are organised according to geographical beats just like on newspapers. Also, *Sky Sports News* journalists have adopted many norms and values that are associated with print reporters, particularly at the tabloid, popular end of the spectrum. *Sky Sports News* journalists focus primarily on breaking exclusive sports stories and cultivating contacts in a similar way to newspaper reporters. These similarities have led to cultural clashes between print and broadcast journalists. For instance, Premier League football club press conferences are now divided into separate print and broadcast sections over concerns that a single briefing benefited broadcasters, who could instantly disseminate material, leaving newspapers with no original content.

Attitudes towards regulation, then, provide an interesting distinction between the two groups of sports journalists. *Sky Sports News* reporters are acutely aware of the Ofcom broadcasting code and there are regular training and briefing sessions within the organisation to ensure they are up-to-speed with latest developments. Broadcast sports journalists use the Ofcom broadcasting code to inform many decisions around their stories. Both awareness and adherence to an ethical code is embedded within the professional culture. A partial explanation can be found in Ofcom's exacting powers providing a deterrent to unethical behaviour with the threat of fines hanging over the newsroom. However, *Sky Sports News* is also concerned with the effects of negative publicity should they be on the wrong side of an Ofcom ruling. Sky is part-owned by Rupert Murdoch and news organisations such as the *Guardian* and *Daily Mail* would relish the opportunity to carry stories of this nature. *Sky Sports News* has regulatory considerations that are specific to the medium of television. These include Ofcom provisions around broadcasters giving prior warning of flashing images (flashlight photography at sports press conferences is a common issue here) for the benefit of viewers with photosensitive epilepsy. Broadcast sports journalists also have to pay particular attention to bad language and violence through Section 1: Protecting the Under-18s, which is a reflection of the earlier point in *McNae's essential law for journalists* about the power of the moving image. On the other hand, the IPSO editors' code of practice is not concerned with bad language and violence.

Sky Sports News reporters must navigate a hyper-commercialised professional sports environment in ensuring that they are compliant with their regulatory code. There is a degree of irony in that Sky has fuelled a highly commercialised sports environment through investing billions of pounds into live television rights – and this, then, creates challenges for journalists working on their 24-hour news channel.

Simon McEnnis   A general shift in sports journalists' source relations has seen direct contact with sports people become a thing of the past due to the intervention of media relations managers and player agents. Instead, sports journalists are primarily dealing with third parties in arranging player access. This move has meant that negotiation has become a key element in sports journalists' daily experiences around which stories to publish, which angle to take and which player they can access. The nature of these discussions invariably moves towards more commercial, promotional elements. Access is often negotiated through *quid-pro-quo* arrangements that often involve sponsorship and marketing personnel. Professional sports people have lucrative sponsorship arrangements that require them to publicise the product. Further, sponsors organise and stage story-gathering opportunities for journalists such as golf days and product launch events.

Sky Sports News programming is seen as a powerful and attractive marketing vehicle by commercial organisations that allows for the bypassing of traditional advertising structures. Further, brands want to be imbued with the authority and endorsement of *Sky Sports News* journalism. *Sky Sports News* journalists would be in breach of their ethical code if they acceded to these demands in a similar manner to their print counterparts. Broadcast journalists continuously resist moves to influence their reporting. These attempts include prominent advertising in the background of camera shots, logos featured prominently on sports clothing, and promotional details of particular charities and services. Television interviews frequently contain sponsors' logos in the background but these are considered acceptable by Ofcom because they feature multiple brand names so no one company is 'unduly prominent'.

Broadcast sports journalists' ethical challenges in resisting editorial interference are further complicated by newspapers entering into copy approval arrangements with the same sources within professional sports. *Sky Sports News* journalists frequently have to educate sponsorship, marketing and public relations personnel on undue prominence and the differences between the regulation of print and television. It would certainly be a relief to broadcast reporters if these sources had a greater awareness and understanding of the Ofcom broadcasting code.

Internally, the *Sky Sports* newsroom needs to be careful around promotional content of other products such as mobile app services and betting. There are also potential issues involving sponsored content. For instance, Ofcom rebuked *Sky Sports* in 2011 following a viewer complaint for featuring an EA Sports sponsorship logo too prominently in its live televising of a football match between Everton and Manchester United (Banham 2011).

Further, broadcast sports journalists struggle with the internal politics of their organisation as part of a wider conflict of interest involving sports rights. Boyle (2006) notes that broadcast sports news is largely driven by the televised sports event to attract audience interest. There are also concerns that broadcasters are primarily seen as media partners with leagues and governing bodies. Therefore, stories surrounding these sports and competitions will be a source of conflict if they are considered as being represented negatively. Broadcast newsrooms can come under pressure from both the rights sellers and their own commercial departments not to run particular stories. It raises the question to what extent broadcast newsrooms should follow journalistic or corporate values. Conflict of interest is undoubtedly a considerable area of ethical concern for broadcast sports journalists but there is nothing in Ofcom's regulatory code that warns against biases in story selection and editorial policy.

Conclusion

This analysis has found that print sports desks trade editorial independence for access to high-profile sports people because the commercial imperative is prioritised over ethical considerations and there is no deterrent provided by their regulatory code. Newspapers believe they have no choice in their story negotiations and that it is the only way they can attract readers to sports sections. Further, they consider their main battle for autonomy to be one of resisting state intervention rather than corporate influence. In this respect, freedom of the press means freedom to make unethical deals with corporate organisations.

On the other hand, broadcast sports journalists consider autonomy in terms of corporate intervention as they are regulated by the state. *Sky Sports News* reporters find that staying compliant with their regulatory code in the area of commercial references and undue prominence is effectively a daily struggle. It also largely defines their relations with marketing, public relations and sponsorship personnel and, therefore, their daily routines.

This study also demonstrated that broadcast sports journalism is an area of the occupation that warrants greater study and analysis. But in focusing on a particular national context it is certainly not universally applicable. For instance, broadcast sports journalists in the US are not so tightly regulated and commercial relationships and prominent sponsorship are an integral and accepted part of the live sports viewing experience. Similarly, there is little protection for objective journalism with partisanship a feature of the televised news landscape as, for instance, on the right-leaning Fox News (also part of the Rupert Murdoch empire). The US context perhaps suggests that UK regulation plays an important role in ensuring the ethical conduct of broadcast journalists.

Simon McEnnis

Future research into sports reporting in the UK needs to take into account the different ethical considerations amongst print and broadcast journalists. The study of sports journalists and digital ethics can also use this analysis as a yardstick into how these issues play out in the traditional (print and broadcast) media. Moreover, future research could analyse the ethical decision-making of BBC sports journalists and compare with the findings of this study. Further, this study has used a tabloid newspaper as its case study and the findings, then, are not necessarily reflective of other print organisations.

Previous research into sports journalism has found that there are clear differences in other aspects of professional culture involving broadsheet and print sports journalists. The *Sun* and *Sky Sports News* have multiple digital offerings beyond their core provision of newspaper and television station respectively. How do traditional and historically embedded notions of ethics transpose to digital environments that are not so tightly regulated. What new ethical challenges are emerging? What are the daily work experiences of online sports journalists in relation to broadcasting codes? The growing complexity of regulation and ethics within different types of sports journalism is a useful indicator of a fragmented professional culture more generally.

Declaration of interest

The author receives no personal financial gain from either news organisations covered in this research.

References

Aldridge, Meryl and Evetts, Julia (2003) Rethinking the concept of professionalism: The case of journalism, *British Journal of Sociology*, Vol. 54, No. 4 pp 542-564

Banham, Mark (2011) Sky Sports warned over on-screen EA branding. Available online at https://www.campaignlive.co.uk/article/sky-sports-warned-on-screen-ea-branding/1053476, accessed on 28 November 2017

Boyle, Raymond (2006) *Sports journalism: Context and issues*, London, Sage

Boyle, Raymond and Haynes, Richard (2009) *Power play: Sport, the media and popular culture*, Edinburgh, University of Edinburgh Press

Boyle, Raymond and Hutchins, Brett (2017) A community of practice: Sport journalism, mobile media and institutional change, *Digital Journalism*, Vol. 5, No. 4 pp 496-512

Boyle, Raymond, Rowe, David and Whannel, Garry (2009) Delight in trivial controversy? Questions for sports journalism, Allan, Stuart (ed.) *The Routledge companion to news and journalism*, London, Routledge pp 245-255

Conlan, Tara (2008) ITV fined record £5.65m. over phone-ins. Available online at https://www.theguardian.com/media/2008/may/08/itv, accessed on 28 November 2017

Deuze, Mark (2005) What is journalism? Professional identity and ideology of journalists reconsidered, *Journalism*, Vol. 6, No. 4 pp 442-464

Hanna, Mark and Dodd, Mike (2016) *McNae's essential law for journalists*, Oxford, Oxford University Press, twenty-third edition

Harcup, Tony (2015) *Journalism: Principles and practice*, London, Sage, third edition

Hutchins, Brett and Rowe, David (2012) *Sport beyond television: The internet, digital media and the rise of networked sport*, London, Routledge

Independent Press Standards Organisation (IPSO) Editors' code of practice. Available online at https://www.ipso.co.uk/editors-code-of-practice/ accessed on 27 November 2017

Kelner, Martin (2013) Sky Sports News' Andy Cairns: 'Journalism is at the top of our agenda'. Available online at https://www.theguardian.com/media/2013/nov/03/sky-sports-news-andy-cairns, accessed on 27 November 2017

McEnnis, Simon (2013) Raising our game: Effects of citizen journalism on Twitter for professional identity and working practices of British sport journalists, *International Journal of Sport Communication*. Vol. 6, No. 4 pp 423-433

McEnnis, Simon (2015) Following the action: How live bloggers are reimagining the professional ideology of sport journalism. *Journalism Practice*, Vol. 10, No. 8 pp 967-982

McEnnis, Simon (2016) Playing on the same pitch: Attitudes of sports journalists towards fan bloggers, *Digital Journalism*, Vol. 5, No. 5 pp 549-566

McEnnis, Simon (2018) Sports Journalism and cultural authority in the digital age, Carter, Tom, Burdsey, Dan and Doidge, Mark (eds) *Transforming power games*, London, Routledge pp 207-219

McGuire, John and Murray, Ray (2013) Attitudes of sport print journalists about developing electronic media skills: A case study of two major newspapers, *International Journal of Sport Communication*, Vol. 6, No. 4 pp 464-477

McGuire, John and Murray, Ray (2016) New work demands create inequity for sports journalists, *Newspaper Research Journal*, Vol. 37, No. 1 pp 58-69

Office of Communications (Ofcom) Broadcasting code. Available online at https://www.ofcom.org.uk/__data/assets/pdf_file/0005/100103/broadcast-code-april-2017.pdf, accessed on 27 November 2017

Rowe, David (2004) *Sport, culture and the media: The unruly trinity*, Buckingham, Open University Press, second edition

Steen, Rob (2014) *Sports journalism: A multimedia primer*, London, Routledge

Sugden, John and Tomlinson, Alan (2007) Stories from planet football and sportsworld: Source relations and collusion in sport journalism, *Journalism Practice*, Vol. 1, No. 1 pp 44-61

Sugden, John and Tomlinson, Alan (2010) What Beckham had for breakfast: The rolling menu of 24/7 sports news, Cushion, Stephen and Lewis, Justin (eds) *The rise of 24-hour news television: Global perspectives*, New York, Peter Lang pp 151-166

Whannel, Garry (1992) *Fields in vision: Television sport and cultural transformation*, London, Routledge

White, Sharon (2017) Effective regulation of the BBC – putting audiences first. Available online at https://www.ofcom.org.uk/about-ofcom/latest/media/speeches/2017/effective-regulation-of-the-bbc-putting-audiences-first, accessed on 28 November 2017

Note on the contributor

Simon McEnnis is principal lecturer in journalism at the University of Brighton. Simon researches into sports journalism as a professional project. He is particularly interested in the increasing complexity and fragmentation of sports journalists as an occupational group. He also examines how sports journalists safeguard their professional interests, particularly on social media. Simon has contributed to special issues on sports journalism in the *International Journal of Sport Communication* and *Digital Journalism* and has made a series of contributions to the *Conversation* website. He has also presented at annual conferences hosted by the North American Society for the Sociology of Sport (NASSS) and the Association for Journalism Education (AJE).

Tracie Edmondson

'Guess and go': The ethics of the mediatisation of professional sport in Australia

This paper highlights ways that changes in the emerging digitised media and communication landscape that envelopes professional sport in Australia influence the ethics of journalism practice. The approach was adopted in the context of mediatisation research as a study of the 'transformation of everyday life, culture and society in the context of the transformation of the media' (Krotz 2017: 108-109). It uses the notion of mediatisation to help conceptualise media change and the Media, Entertainment and Arts Alliance's Journalist Code of Ethics as a benchmark for ethical practices in Australia. Findings indicate that routine violations of core ethical standards of Australian journalism – such as 'striving for accuracy', doing the 'utmost to give a fair opportunity for reply' and achieving 'fair correction of errors' – are occurring as a result of the pervasive digitised 24/7 news cycle (MEAA Journalist Code of Ethics 2017).

Key words: mediatisation, sport communicators, journalism, digitised media

Introduction: Sport matters
Research into the field of sports communication is important because sport in Australia matters – economically, culturally and socially. Figures bear out the importance of sport to lifestyles in the country. More than 11 million Australians aged 15 years and over (60 per cent of the population) participate in sport and physical recreation (Australian Bureau of Statistics 2013-2014); almost 8 million attend live sporting events each year and millions more consume sport on television or other electronic devices; many communities and charities receive funds from sport; significant corporations attach themselves to sport in sponsor arrangements; millions of dollars are injected into the economy from major sporting events; and sport makes various contributions to the overall wellbeing of society (Stewart 2017). Sport makes a difference.

Sport plays an integral part in the lives of Australians. ... Our participation in and passion for sport creates significant benefits for Australia. The sector's economic contribution is equivalent to 2-3 per cent of GDP, employing more than 220,000 people and attracting 1.8 million volunteers – Australia's largest volunteer destination (Australian Sports Commission 2017: 4).

These statistics highlight that sport in Australia is big business and it is important to the 'lifeworlds' (Frandsen 2015: 3) of citizens. Therefore, how sports organisations communicate and interact with their various stakeholders is important.

High profile sports have a close relationship with media and the changes in the media landscape over the past 20 years have challenged practitioners managing sports communication. The changes have also provided opportunities, enabling professional sports organisations to engage more directly with their fans across multiple platforms and channels, live and interactive.

PAPER

But while sports fans in Australia are more connected than ever before, it is not enough. A report into the future of sport in Australia produced by the Gemba Group explains that 'sport is entertainment and entertainment is sport' (2017: 13-14), with fans craving intimate access to their lives away from the arena with behind-the-scenes footage and content. As Rob Mills, CEO of the Gemba Group, comments:

> The lines between sport and entertainment have blurred beyond recognition. Sport fans now demand non-stop entertainment, full immersion and unfettered access to athletes, teams and events. Digital technologies and increased connectivity is at the core of this revolution (ibid: 2).

At the same time as sports fans are demanding more personalised content about their sporting heroes that often has little to do with their prowess in the sporting arena, complaints against media organisations are rising. The government regulator of broadcasting, the Australian Communications and Media Authority (ACMA), has found citizens are particularly concerned about industry behaviour centred around accuracy, fair treatment and privacy (ACMA 2011: 40-60).

This paper examines the influence of changes to the media and communication environment that have accompanied digitisation on the ethical standards of journalism practices in relation to sport coverage. It focuses, in particular, on the perspectives of sport media practitioners working for peak sport organisations in Australia, drawing data from a series of in-depth interviews.

Tracie Edmondson

Background
As a practitioner with a career in the media-sport industry spanning 32 years, I have worked in various sports journalism and sports media manager roles and more recently in senior communications executive positions in professional sports organisations. I was motivated to study the changing media landscape and how it has influenced practice in Australia. I started as part of a generation of Australian media professionals who were members of the MEAA and practised attentively according to the guidelines. I have used the MEAA Journalist Code of Ethics in this study to consider what is and is not ethical in today's changed media landscape from the perspective of sports communication professionals (SCP) and senior executives (SE) in professional sports organisations.

From my experiences and observations, I am interested in exploring strategies for managing the issues and implications around the media's need for more unique content, more often and more quickly than ever before – the race to be first with content, with seconds not hours to verify facts and sources; the type of content being pursued given the greater demands of the 24/7 news cycle with less traditional journalistic resources; and the 'flattening' of the media-sport hierarchy, whereby the 'content of sport is no longer controlled and distributed by traditional-media organisations' (Gibbs and Hayne 2013: 406).

One way of conceptualising changes to the media environment is as mediatisation. This paper's approach draws on Scandinavian concepts of mediatisation in sport (Frandsen 2013; 2015) and modeling of responses to mediatisation (Brandii et al. 2011; Donges and Jarren 2014), and aims to study how changes in the media have transformed 'everyday life, culture and society' (Krotz 2017: 108-109). This approach has support from other researchers, with the concept of the theory of mediatisation, as specified by Krotz and others, identified as a 'promising candidate' (Eberwein and Porlezza 2016: 338) to provide a theoretical framework for the empirical study of communication and media ethics.

> From the perspective of communication and media ethics, which is struggling to cope with the current transformations of the media, mediatization theory seems to be a valuable vehicle which can help to differentiate the determining factors of this process of change, thus also outlining the key fields of discourse of a future digital media ethics (Eberwein and Porlezza 2016: 338).

Defining mediatisation
The framework for my study and the research question that guides it are based on an adaptation of Frandsen's (2015) empirical study of national sports federations in Denmark, which explores mediatisation

through Donges' 'three central dimensions: perception, structure and behavior' to understand how organisations have responded to 'media-induced change' (Brandii et al. 2011: 7). Frandsen's study found 'digital media are a major concern across organisations' and many 'struggle' and are 'in a state of flux' with the 'new wave of mediatization' (Frandsen 2015: 1).

Among the criticisms facing researchers using the concept of mediatisation is that it lacks a clear and unified definition. Contributing to the confusion around a clear definition is the reference to two traditions or approaches of mediatisation – the institutionalist tradition and the social-constructivist (Couldry and Hepp 2013: 5; Deacon and Stanyer 2014: 1033). Hepp and Couldry (2010) suggest the differing approaches highlight that mediatisation means different things in different contexts so, therefore, it will have different definitions; while others (Ekstrom et al. 2016: 1097) describe the differing positions around a definition of mediatisation as a sign of the field's 'maturation'.

The institutionalist approach to mediatisation is seen as a process whereby different social fields or systems (like politics, religion or sport) conform to the rules or 'media logic' (Altheide and Snow 1979) of the media as an independent institution. These non-media actors are believed to do so in order to perform successfully in the (mass) media (Couldry et al. 2013: 5).

In contrast, the traditional social-constructivist approach to mediatisation refers to the role of the media in the process of the communicative construction of social reality whereby the ever-changing information and communication technologies are driving change (ibid; Krotz 2009) Therefore, the use and meaning of the word 'media' differs in each tradition. It is believed that while these differing traditions have co-existed for some time, they have come closer together in recent years (Couldry et al. 2013: 5), which helps to respond to criticism of the mediatisation concept, with perceived opposition between the two traditions described as 'counter-productive' (Ekstrom et al. 2016: 1098).

This shared view has evolved since the concept of mediatisation was first applied to 'media's impact on political communication and other effects on politics' (Hjarvard 2008: 106), to more recently constituting 'an organizing principle for other spheres of life' (Livingstone and Lunt 2014: 706). Hjarvard's (2008: 105) early view of mediatisation defined it as a 'theory of the influence media exert on society and culture', but he now describes it as a double structure where media at the end of the 20th century 'have both become integrated in the operations of other social institutions and cultural spheres, while also acquiring the status of social institutions in their own right' (ibid: 17).

Tracie Edmondson

Though there are many different definitions of mediatisation, I am for now adopting the interpretation by Krotz (2017) that best describes and frames the concept I am using for this paper. His definition is based on the transformation of the 'media system' from one that consisted of unique media and media groups to the current digital computer-controlled infrastructure which is 'less oriented by journalistic rules and more by economic rules' and has changed the 'human communication environment in a fundamental way' (ibid: 104-105).

> Therefore, it is necessary to study, besides the transformation of media, a second transformation: the transformation of everyday life, culture and society in the context of the transformation of the media – which, in the long run, organizes all symbolic operations of a society and culture in that digital computer-controlled infrastructure, consisting of networks of computers (ibid: 105).

Research question

This paper explores the findings of the interviews conducted and reflects on the ethical issues and implications for sports news and communication of the new media landscape that includes sports digital and social platforms such as websites, Twitter and Facebook. The research question to be addressed in this paper is: what are communicator perceptions of the influence of digitised news practices on MEAA standards in sports journalism?

Method

The study used qualitative in-depth semi-structured interviews with sports communication professionals (SCP) and senior executives (SE) of major sport bodies. Interview participants were recruited through a combination of online organisational research, personal contacts, emails and follow-up phone calls.

The initial sampling framework was to include all staff working in senior media or communications roles and senior executives in major professional sports leagues in Australia and the national governing bodies for those leagues. Sampling was both purposive and convenient. Participants were selected based on a combination of selection criteria and availability within the timescale of the study in the cities I travelled to. One key criteria for participants was that they had worked in the media-sport industry for at least 8 to 10 years (before 2009) because my major study's focus is on the changing nature of media-sport interactions in an age of digital mediatisation. A person with only few years in the industry 'lacks the historical perspective needed to explain' ways media in the digital age have changed the nature of media-sport interactions (Gibbs and Haynes 2013: 397).

For the purpose of my study, professional sport in Australia refers to the national sporting competitions for elite professional teams, with full-time professional athletes. The seven sports leagues/ competitions that satisfied the criteria, have multi-million dollar broadcast rights deals with live broadcast of all matches, either via free-to-air, subscription TV and live streaming or a combination of methods. Six other national leagues were overlooked because their athletes were either semi-professional in terms of payment and/or the leagues did not receive full live broadcast of all matches.

From the seven professional sports leagues chosen, the sample widened to include all of the 65 national league teams and the seven governing bodies. The study set a target of interviewing the SCP and a SE from the same seven national league teams and SCP and a SE from the seven identified national governing bodies for those leagues for a total of 28 interviews. A further criterion was set to include representatives from all of the major states and the Australian Capital Territory to ensure the study was truly national. This proved a challenge in selecting the 14 interview participants from the national league teams because of the concentration of teams on the east coast of Australia in Queensland, New South Wales and Victoria.

PAPER

Participants were approached by email and phone to determine if they were interested in participating and interviews scheduled. Interview guidelines were prepared and tested in a trial study. See Table 1 for participant demographics.

TABLE 1: Interview Participant Demographics

PARTICIPANT NO.	SPORT	EXPERIENCE* RANGE (YRS)	AGE RANGE	GENDER
1	Rugby league	20-29	40-49	M
2	Cricket	20-29	40-49	F
3	Rugby League	40-49	50-59	M
4	Rugby league	20-29	50-59	M
5	Netball	20-29	50-59	F
6	Netball	10-19	30-39	F
7	Cricket	30-39	50-59	M
8	Soccer	10-19	50-59	M
9	Soccer	10-19	30-39	M
10	Australian rules football	20-29	50-59	M
11	Rugby union	8-10	40-49	M
12	Soccer	30-39	50-59	M
13	Cricket	30-39	50-59	M
14	Australian rules football	20-29	40-49	M

Tracie
Edmondson

15	Basketball	20-29	50-59	M
16	Soccer	8-10	50-59	M
17	Basketball	8-10	20-29	M
18	Netball	8-10	20-29	F
19	Rugby union	10-19	40-49	M
20	Rugby league	10-19	50-59	M
21	Netball	20-29	50-59	F
22	Basketball	10-19	30-39	M
23	Rugby union	10-19	50-59	M
24	Cricket	30-39	50-59	M
25	Australian rules football	30-39	60-69	M
26	Australian rules football	20-29	50-59	F

Number of years of experience in sport and/or media industries/studies

A total of 26 of a proposed 28 semi-structured in-depth, qualitative interviews were conducted between 31 May 2017 and 7 September 2017 as the primary source of data collection using Rubin and Rubin's (2005) 'responsive interviewing' model. Interviews were conducted by phone (calls to Perth, Adelaide, Canberra, Melbourne and Brisbane) and in person (Sydney, Melbourne and Brisbane) with interviews ranging in length from 40 minutes to two hours. Over the May to September period, two respondents left their jobs and I was unable to interview their replacements in that timeframe.

Interviews and observation notes were transcribed and a two-step process of coding, using methods set out by Saldana (2016) was applied. In brief, this process involved initial descriptive coding, followed by process coding. The analysis reported here required researcher familiarity with the spirit and practice of the MEAA Journalist Code of Ethics (2017). The researcher coded the interview scripts (words and ideas), interpreting journalist practices and coverage outcomes discussed, in terms of alignment or deviation from the code of journalism ethics (see MEAA Journalist Code of Ethics 2017).

Respondents were guaranteed confidentiality so individual names and organisations are not used in the paper.

Findings and discussion
The interviews revealed profound concerns for ethical sports journalism practice arising from what is referred to as mediatisation. These findings report three main trends affecting the spirit of the code centred around the drive for more unique content, more often, more quickly to satisfy the 24/7 news cycle demands for both traditional media (newspapers, television and radio) and

new media (digital and social including website, online, Facebook, Twitter, etc):

- rising complaints with increased technology;
- less resources but more content;
- accuracy a casualty of speed.

All interview participants agreed the rapidly changing media landscape offered both opportunities and challenges. Opportunities include the ability to communicate directly with stakeholders on multiple platforms and greater control over messaging. It has also created greater opportunities for older, more experienced sports communication professionals in senior communication management roles in sporting organisations, while opening up a multitude of digital, social and other media roles for younger media and communication workers in these organisations.

PAPER

Sports organisations are less reliant on traditional broadcast media organisations to communicate with stakeholders with participants agreeing the media-sport hierarchy has flattened and media power has reduced, a phenomenon referred to by Gibbs et al. (2013: 406) in their finding that the one-way traditional model of communication is now a 'two-way mode of communication that represents a form of departure from traditional media models'. At the same time, traditional media and relationships with media are still viewed as being as important, if not more so for some participants:

> One of the newspapers' big problems is ... they're in this fog where they think they set the agenda, everything they say is what it is all about. That's bullshit, that's not true anymore. Well certainly not to the degree it was 10 or 20 years ago ... no way in the world. Participant 1

> Is it click bait? What do they want? What's happened also, though, is the public aren't stupid so the power of traditional media is diminished. So the ability to influence is not as great as it was as well. Participant 10

Increased technology, rising complaints

A report into digital Australians has linked complaints about media to technology, with audience and reader complaints about the media in Australia rising significantly (Harding-Smith 2011: 11). The two main bodies that handle public complaints on Australian media have experienced huge increases in the number of complaints over the past 10-20 years:

- 57 per cent in five years (2006-2011) for the government regulator of broadcasting, the Australian Communications and Media Authority (ACMA), and

Tracie
Edmondson

- 42 per cent above the long-term average (1990-2011) for the newspaper self-regulator, the Australian Press Council (APC) (Harding-Smith 2011: 1).

In the six years since the Harding-Smith report, the APC has recorded a further 24 per cent increase in complaints from the public to more than 700 complaints per year (up from 399 in 2011) (APC 2017). The Harding-Smith report (2011:1) also found that, despite the internet providing Australians with a multitude of alternative news and information sources, the public still consumes news from within the pre-existing media ecosystem. All but one of the 12 news sites in Australia's top 100 most visited sites are owned by major existing media outlets (of those, eight are owned by News Limited and Fairfax).

A key concern that media standards are most likely to slip when media organisations are under financial pressure was reinforced with findings that the media industry is not conforming to best practice standards for industry self-regulation as recommended by the Australian federal government (Harding-Smith: 15). Attitudinal research by the ACMA (Digital Australians 2011: 40-60) also found key citizen concerns about industry behaviour centred around accuracy in news and current affairs, fair treatment and privacy, transparency and balance in advertising and programming, preventing harm particularly to children and effective complaints-handling mechanisms.

> Four in five online Australians agreed that it is important for Australian news organisations to check facts before publishing a news story online and 77 per cent thought it was important for the websites of Australian television broadcasters to have the same rules about accuracy and fairness as do news items shown on television (ACMA 2011).

The ACMA found privacy concerns had increased, in particular around 'material taken surreptitiously with mobile phones and material that has been harvested from social media sites without the consent of the subject' (Chapman 2015).

These trends highlight that during a time when technology has transformed the media system, the everyday practice of the sports journalist has also been transformed, indicating behaviours that do not reflect the requirements of the MEAA Journalist Code of Ethics.

However, the MEAA, which sets the standard for journalists in Australia, has made no changes to its Code of Ethics for journalists in almost 20 years. Originally established as the Australian Journalists Association (AJA) in Melbourne in 1910, the Journalist Code of Ethics was established in 1944 – an initiative prompted by similar codes in US and Britain. The code was reviewed and updated in 1984, subject to a major review in 1994, and further updated in 1999 with the current MEAA Journalist Code of Ethics instituted.

The MEAA does not believe the code needs further updating to reflect changes in technology, arguing 'the requirements of ethical journalism do not alter from one platform to another or one technology to another' (MEAA Journalist Code of Ethics 2017: 2). But some sports communicators disagree.

> They're putting old school thinking across new – especially young people – new ways of behaviour. Participant 10

The self-regulating code lists its values as honesty, fairness, independence and respect for others, which are further reflected in the Code's 12 standards. This paper will focus on the values reflected in two key standards:

> Standard 1: Report and interpret honestly, *striving for accuracy*, *fairness* and disclosure of all essential facts. Do not suppress relevant available facts, or give distorting emphasis. Do your *utmost to give a fair opportunity for reply*.

> Standard 12: Do your *utmost to achieve fair correction of errors* (MEAA Journalist Code of Ethics 2017).

Participants interviewed experienced behaviours from journalists that were not in keeping with the spirit of the these MEAA standards, with key contributing factors associated with the diminishing staff levels at traditional media organisations, despite a higher demand for content and the desperation to be first with the news, putting speed before accuracy.

Less resources, more content
Sports communicators emphasised greater control over their messaging across a range of channels and platforms than ever before, but reported fewer traditional (and experienced) journalists, producing more content because of a greater focus on online, digital and social media. This was in contrast to staff resources in media and communication roles within Australian professional sport which were perceived to be increasing in response to the changing media landscape.

> The big problem now is they want more now and they have less. Resources have become a real problem for them. And it's just changed their attitude towards things. And I think social media has been the killer for that, for them. Participant 1

Participants experienced issues with fundamental MEAA journalistic ethics of accuracy and fairness as a result of the decreasing number of journalists in traditional media organisations – and, in particular, less experienced sports journalists – to write, produce and edit the content. Many believe this is leading to poor quality of reporting.

> I've always thought the way out of diminishing sales is to increase the quality of the product, not decrease it. But they've dumbed it down, rather than saying our point of difference is quality. They don't even try. It's a race to the bottom. It is a race to the bottom and there's no way out of it, is there? And the young journos aren't getting grounded well enough. There's just such a rush. Participant 10

> Most of the media that has gone online is still traditional media, but the quality of journalism, through cost-saving, diminishing resources and the youthfulness of the people that are coming in, is diminished. Participant 3

> I think it's also part of standards of what media companies are prepared to accept and publish. It is so much lower than it has ever been. Participant 14

Participants believed young journalists, who have replaced senior sports journalists in shrinking news rooms, are not taking time to build relationships with contacts in sports organisations and are happy to burn contacts; while CEOs, coaches and players do not know the new young reporters and are not sure they can trust them.

> So the old days remember where players had relationships with media are almost completely gone … because they don't have the interaction they used to. … Some players are more wary so they are not opening up as much. But journos are also just as willing to shelve blokes because they don't know them. Participant 1

> The other thing that's the problem is everyone's so rushed the opportunity to build relationships with the journos, the player and the club is harder as well. They don't have the time to sit down to build that rapport. It's frustrating. Participant 10

Participants also believed competition for fewer jobs is greater, leading to a greater focus on celebrity-style reporting.

> Also what's happening with young people coming in, they're looking to go up the tree as fast as they can so they're trying to impress, which impacts again on … they don't care, they just want to be able to show that they're relevant rather than getting it right. Participant 10

> I think the problem is that the new breed coming through is going to be more scandal-related than football-related. You

don't have the young guys coming through, spending years and years going to games, getting to know the coach, getting to know the players. So the young guys come in now and ... the quickest way to the top is to bring a scandal. Participant 3

Participants believe the new media landscape has blurred the lines between journalists working in a professional capacity for a media organisation and those working as individuals, with multiple platforms to express their opinions. This is even more of an issue for those journalists working with multiple hats – as a journalist for their newspaper, a sideline eye for a radio station, as a guest/host on a TV sports chat show, producing personal blogs and/or podcasts and running a Twitter handle that states the views expressed are their own:

> It's a bit of a mind trap both for administrators and media managers [because] they never know if what they are saying is on the record or off the record because they never know if they're talking to a journalist acting in a professional capacity or someone who just has an opinion and they now have an audience and a platform to be able to express that opinion whenever it suits them. Participant 22

Accuracy a casualty of speed

The speed of the contemporary news cycle – a matter of seconds not hours – has also contributed to the violation of the MEAA Journalist Code of Ethics to strive for accuracy and a fair opportunity to reply, with interview participants perceiving the desperate drive for content and, in particular, the race to be first being put above checking facts, being key issues.

> They just guess and go ... 15 years ago, or 10 years ago an editor would have said: 'Are you sure about this?' It doesn't matter now. If it's sexy it goes. They're not really concerned about being right or wrong. Participant 1

> They're rushing out to Twitter to get their version out that they're the first, even though the public doesn't care who's first, which is stunning. Participant 10

> ... they're so desperate now that they don't ever do the 'right thing' [in quotes] anymore. They just do whatever they think they have to. They don't care. Participant 1

Participants agreed this was being compounded by a 24/7 news operation that recycles other news stories, without checking the accuracy or doing their utmost to give a fair opportunity to reply. Retractions are rarely given and, if they are, it is not with the same prominence as the initial offending story.

Tracie Edmondson

We often ask people to correct things but you know quite often the damage is done … and they think that their liability or their culpability rather can be overcome by simply correcting it in an online story that's already been read a thousand times and has been saved or reprinted or whatever it might be. Participant 22

I think it's just about getting people looking at it even if it's wrong, then we deal with it tomorrow if it's wrong and just say we'll sort of fix it, but they don't. Participant 3

The findings highlight that, regardless of how the media system has been transformed, there is an expectation for sports journalists to uphold the values of the MEAA Journalist Code of Ethics, but an acknowledgement, and almost acceptance, that it isn't always the case.

Findings suggest that the old school values of the MEAA Journalist Code of Ethics are as important as ever in the new media landscape and ignoring these values could be damaging for sports journalism as a profession. Some participants agree the public is more discerning, with more information available to form an opinion and more platforms to voice their opinion in the contemporary media environment:

The public might not like us all the time, but they don't like the journalists more of the time. Participant 3

Criticism has even come from within the journalism profession for unethical use in particular of Twitter in mainstream reporting, with a journalist from *The Australian* demanding better if journalism is to rebuild public confidence as a profession.

Journalists are supposed to offer audiences some meaning in the midst of this mess … For journalism and media organisations to stand out from the crowd they need to be the source of reliable, verified and concise information and opinion based on proven facts – something we used to call 'truth' … some prominent journalists seem to have formed the view that Twitter is so different that they have a licence to ignore some of the foundation stones of their ethical codes (Pearson 2012).

Limitations
Widening this study to include the perception of sports journalists (like Pearson) about the MEAA Journalist Code of Ethics – what they know of; how they became aware of it; do they follow it; and do they think it needs changing – would provide a useful and practical perspective. This could include considering the role of the gatekeeper and who is ultimately responsible for determining what it and is not ethical in today's changed media landscape.

Conclusion

The preliminary findings presented in this paper contribute to the limited literature on mediatisation and sport in Australia. They also, in part, underpin the significance of a study focused on the everyday management and adaptation of Australian professional sports organisations to the changing media-sport interactions from the perspective of sports communicators. The findings also suggest that further research is needed in this subject; for instance, through a comparative study involving professional sport in the US and UK, which Australian professional sport often uses as a benchmark.

References

AAP (2015) AFL maintains crowd-pulling status, *Australian*, 21 May. Available online at http://www.theaustralian.com.au/sport/afl/afl-maintains-crowdpulling-status/news-story/b4ca1cc859749bc22ec27169094e4b1c

ACMA (2011) *Digital Australians: Expectations about media content in a converging media environment. Qualitative and quantitative research report.* Available online at https://www.acma.gov.au/-/media/Research-and-Analysis/Information/pdf/Digital-Australians-Expectations-about-media-content-in-a-converging-media-environment.PDF

Altheide, D. and Snow, R. (1979) *Media logic*, Beverley Hills, CA: Sage

Australian Press Council. (2017) Australia. Available online at http://www.presscouncil.org.au/complaints/

Australian Sports Commission (2017) *Intergenerational review of Australian sport*, Boston Consulting Group for Australian Sports Commission

Brandii, M., Donges, P. and Jentges, E. (2011) Media-induced change in political organizations? Interest groups and their reactions to media. Paper presented at 6th ECPR General Conference, Reykjavik, Iceland, 25-27 August

Chapman, C. (2015) Address to the Australian Press Council. 27 November 2015. Available online at http://www.presscouncil.org.au/uploads/52321/ufiles/Chris_Chapman_Press_Council_Address_-_27_November_2015_-_FINAL.pdf

Couldry, N. (2012) *Media society, world: Social theory and digital media practice*, Cambridge, Polity Press

Couldry, N. and Hepp, A. (2013) Conceptualising mediatization: Contexts, traditions, arguments, *Communication Theory*, Vol. 23, No. 3 pp 191-202

Deacon, D. and Stanyer, J. (2014) Mediatization: Key concept or conceptual bandwagon, *Media, Culture & Society*, Vol. 36, No. 7 pp 1032–1044

Donges, P. and Jarren, O. (2014) Mediatization of political organizations: Changing parties and interest groups? Esser, F. and Stromback, J. (eds) *Mediatization of politics: Understanding the transformation of Western democracies*, London, Palgrave Macmillan

Eberwein, T. and Porlezza, C. (2016) Both sides of the story: Communication ethics in mediatized worlds, *Journal of Communication*, Vol. 66 pp 328-342

Ekstrom, M., Fornas, J., Jansson, A. and Jerslev, A. (2016) Three tasks for mediatization research: Contributions to an open agenda, *Media, Culture & Society*, Vol. 38, No. 7 pp 1090-1108

Frandsen, K. (2015) Sports organizations in a new wave of mediatization, *Communication & Sport*, Vol. 4, No. 4 pp 1-16

Frandsen, K. (2013) *Mediatization of sports organizations: Approaching changes on a meso-level.* Paper presented at NordMedia, Oslo, 8-11 August

Gemba Group (2017) *NBN Future of sport report: The revolution in digital sports consumption.* Available online at https://www.nbnco.com.au/content/dam/nbnco2/documents/2017-nbn-Report%20Design-FA-future-of-sport-HR.pdf

PAPER

Tracie
Edmondson

Gibbs, C. and Haynes, R. (2013) A phenomenological investigation into how Twitter has changed the nature of sport media relations, *International Journal of Sport Communication*, Vol. 6 pp 394-408

Harding-Smith, R. (2011) *Media ownership and regulation in Australia*, Sydney: Centre for Policy Development. Available online at https://cpd.org.au/wp-content/uploads/2011/11/Centre_for_Policy_Development_Issue_Brief.pdf

Hepp, A. and Couldry, N. (2010) Media events in globalized media cultures, Couldry,N., Hepp, A. and Krotz, F. (eds) *Media events in a global age*, London, Routledge pp 1-20

Hepp, A., Hjarvard, S. and Lundby, K. (2015) Mediatization; Theorizing the Interplay between media, culture and society, *Media, Culture and Society*, Vol. 37, No. 2 pp 314-322

Hjarvard, S. (2008) The mediatization of society: A theory of the media as agents of social and cultural change, *Nordicom Review*, Vol. 29 pp 105-134

Hjarvard, S. (2013) *The mediatization of culture and society*, London, Routledge

Krotz, F. (2009) Mediatization: A concept with which to grasp media and societal change, Lundby, K. (ed.) *Mediatization: Concept, changes, consequences*, New York, Peter Lang pp 19-38

Krotz, F. (2017) Explaining the mediatisation approach, *Javnost: The Public*, Vol. 24, No. 2 pp 103-118

Livingstone, S. and Lunt, P. (2014) Mediatization: An emerging paradigm for media and communication studies, Lundby, K. (ed.) *Mediatization of communication: Handbooks of Communication Sciences*, No. 21, Berlin, deGruyter

MEAA (2017) Journalist Code of Ethics, Australia. Available online at https://www.meaa.org/meaa-media/code-of-ethics/

Pearson, M. (2012) Media twitters as Murdoch fronts Leveson, *Weekend Australian*, 28 April p. 12

Rubin, H. J. and Rubin, I. (2005) *Qualitative interviewing: The art of hearing data*, California, Sage Publications, second edition

Saldana, J. (2016) *The coding manual for qualitative researchers*, London, Sage Publications, third edition

Stewart, B. (2017) Sport is more than just a fringe-player in Australia's economy, *The Conversation*, 25 January. Available online at https://theconversation.com/sport-is-more-than-just-a-fringe-player-in-australias-economy-71212

Note on the contributor

Tracie Edmondson is a sports media communications specialist with 32 years' experience in the sport-media industry having worked as a sports journalist and a senior communications executive in professional sports organisations in Australia. She has also worked on major sporting events including four Olympic Games (2000, 2004, 2012, 2016), two Rugby League World Cups (2008, 2017) and the AFC (soccer) Asian Cup (2015). She is currently working full-time as Head of Public Affairs for New South Wales Rugby League (Australia) and is a doctoral candidate (Communication) at Charles Sturt University, New South Wales, Australia.

Jonathan Cable
Glyn Mottershead

'Can I click it? Yes you can': Football journalism, Twitter and clickbait

This paper is part of an ongoing longitudinal analysis of the Twitter timelines of 15 major football media outlets from 2010 to 2017. It aims to demonstrate how over time the need for content has increased the scale and frequency of tweets, duplication of content and an increased focus on high profile football clubs, players and managers. The use of Twitter in this way is more directed at being a one-directional broadcasting medium, where content is increasingly homogenised – and where search engine optimisation and attractive headlines trump journalistic content. On the most basic of levels clickbait exists to generate traffic, increase site visitors and attract more advertising. As a result, this is reducing the quality of football journalism in a never-ending quest for easy content.

Key words: clickbait, football journalism, social media, sport journalism, Twitter

Introduction

Sport is an integral part of our lives, and how we find out about our favourite athletes, clubs and sports is through sport journalism. The focus of this paper is on the mechanisms used by media outlets to get us to read their sport news on social media, in particular Twitter. Sports journalism is understudied in this respect. There is clearly an ever-increasing competition for the attentions of fragmented audience and, in response, media outlets are resorting to using the techniques of clickbait. The inspiration for this paper comes from the football website *Football365* whose daily eye on the media section entitled 'Mediawatch' presents readers with the press's take on current football issues (*Football365* 2017). This section of their website highlights clear examples of journalistic pandering to draw in audiences and generate clicks. It has regularly exposed the use of Search Engine Optimisation (SEO), clickbait and other journalistic strategies (for work on the use of SEO see Dick 2011).

One such example it highlighted comes from the Twitter feed of *Mail Sport* in March 2016 where it tweeted: 'Man Utd, City, Chelsea, Arsenal & Liverpool chiefs in secret meeting over Euro

Jonathan Cable
Glyn Mottershead

Super League' (*Mail Sport* 2016). Once clicked it is revealed that the meeting related to the International Champions Cup, a pre-season tournament set to be held in America (Gill et al. 2016). What this example illustrates is how clickbait is designed to operate. The headline in this instance did not match the subsequent content. The term clickbait, however, is very contentious and there are several slight variations to its definition. For Chen et al. (2015), clickbait is a symptom of the digital news business model and the thirst for page views. More pointedly, Silverman describes the process of clickbait as the 'tendency for news sites to pair declarative headlines with body text that expresses skepticism about the veracity of the information' (2015). Similarly, Kuiken et al. talk of 'a vague headline that induces curiosity, which is then used to lure readers into clicking on the headline' (2017: 4). These definitions do not necessarily point to the publication of outright lies – rather more key factual differences between headline and body of text.

Chen et al. provide an excellent breakdown to the types of cues and mechanisms utilised in typical clickbait headlines (2015: 5). These range from affective language and action words to forward referencing and reverse narratives (ibid). The mechanisms by which these work span across curiosity piquing, reading enjoyment, generating suspense and emotional appeal (ibid). In addition, there is the technique of 'forward-referencing', identified by Blom and Hansen, which is the way in which a headline gives reference to 'forthcoming (parts of the) discourse relative to the current location in the discourse, e.g. "This is the best news story you will ever read"' (2015: 1). This demonstrates that, while there are differences over the definition of the term 'clickbait', these arguments all highlight clickbait's basic aim of generating clicks. At one end is the use of attractive headlines to generate traffic; at the other is the deliberate publishing of misleading information in a desperate search for reader attention. In the past, a titillating headline on a newspaper may have been called 'readbait', but the current use of clickbait is ultimately deceiving the consumer.

The increase in clickbait stems from changes in the newsroom and journalism practices around social media stemming from the incorporation of analytics software such as Chartbeat. This is a system used in newsrooms by major publishers such as Trinity Mirror, and its use led one of the editors at their *Cornwall Live* website to write an editorial defending the use of ChartBeat against accusations of clickbait (Merrington 2017). In it, Jacqui Merrington states that the ChartBeat screen is 'what makes the newsroom tick' but that this is leading to a culture where the audience is simply given the news they want, rather than information that they need:

> So rather than guessing whether people are reading what we write, we have a pretty good idea based on the figures flashing

on our screen all day every day. And to know whether they like it or not, we get an instant reaction via Facebook or Twitter or through comments on the site (ibid).

Most tellingly, Merrington adds: 'It's not just about "news" any more. It's about informing people, entertaining them, engaging them' (ibid). Given the editor's rationale for the incorporation of this type of technology, there is a sense that it is not a completely clickbait-orientated organisation, but it does highlight the importance of social media in newsrooms today. It follows that these metrics are what the journalists are judged on. The ramifications in terms of content is a shift from public interest journalism to what is of interest to the public, in other words from news to entertainment. The market forces behind giving people what they want remove risk-taking and redefine what journalism is for.

These headlines work because, as psychologist George Loewenstein argues, our brains are hardwired to want to fill in gaps in information created by clickbait:

> Such information gaps produce the feeling of deprivation labelled curiosity. The curious individual is motivated to obtain the missing information to reduce or eliminate the feeling of deprivation (Loewenstein 1994).

If a headline features a cliff-hanger, for instance, then we will be inclined to click because we want to find out the answers. It is this feeling of deprivation which provokes the reader into making these decisions. Take the following for example:

> Five things we have learned from Manchester United's US tour (*Guardian Sport* 2014).

This example is typical of a form of sports article which claims to have uncovered new information through watching a sporting event, in this case football. The headline construction gives none of this new material away. The tweet is, in short, tantalising, a cliff-hanger and points towards a knowledge gap as it gives no answers. All of these are traits of clickbait. It plays on our emotions and impulses which are key in provoking online interaction. Berger and Milkman, in a study about what makes particular content go 'viral' online, highlight article traits containing either 'emotionality, positivity, awe, anger, anxiety, disgust, and sadness' (2011). All of which are characteristics of sports. Social media, on the other hand, is defined as having an underlying 'emotional architecture' exemplified by the 'like' button (Wahl-Jorgensen 2013, see also Bakir and McStay's work on emotion and fake news 2017).

Jonathan Cable
Glyn Mottershead

Methodology

The decision behind focusing on Twitter for this paper is because of its prominent usage among journalists and news outlets in general. A tweet is very similar to a headline in that it is textually dependent on the article it refers to. Traditionally headlines have been considered to be 'a special kind of text; a text which cannot have an autonomous status. It is a text correlated to another text…' (Iarovici and Amel 1989: 441). A tweet, therefore, acts as a sort of headline where the reader needs to choose to click a link before they see the rest of a story.

We sought to look at the different ways in which news outlets tweeted about sport, which tweets received the most engagement in terms of 'likes' and 'favourites', what hashtags were prominent and what were the most frequent combinations of words. To achieve this, we chose 15 Twitter accounts analysing tweets from the date the account opened to 31 March 2017:

Outlet	Twitter Handle
BBC Sport	bbcsport
Daily Express	dexpress_sport
Daily Mail Football	mailfootball
ESPN FC	espnfc
Guardian Sport	guardian_sport
Indy Football	indyfootball
Indy Sport	indysport
Metro Sport	metro_sport
Mirror Football	mirrorfootball
Mirror Sport	mirrorsport
Sky Sports News	skysportsnews
Sun Football	thesunfootball
Sun Sport	sunsport
Telegraph Football	telefootball
Telegraph Sport	telegraphsport

Table 1: List of media outlets in the sample

The Twitter feeds chosen feature both general sport-related accounts as well as some outlets which dedicate an entire feed to just football. The high profile nature of football and especially the English Premier League had a major influence on the results. The implications of this will be discussed further on in this paper. The Twitter API (advanced programming interface) only allows searches to go back 3,200 tweets, meaning that a more limited time frame would be available to create the corpus. To get around this, an open-source Python web scraper (https://github.com/bpb27/

twitter_scraping) was used on each target organisation in turn. This is a two-stage process: the first step automates the Twitter search, using the @username and a date range to find the ID for individual tweets by the target account. This does not require the Twitter API and is not rate limited – it is an automated web scraper.

The second stage to the data-gathering uses the Twitter API to turn the list of IDs returned by stage one into a CSV (spreadsheet) of tweets for the account which has the following headers: favourite_count, source, text, in_reply_to_screen_name, is_retweet, created_at, retweet_count, id_str. The API method for getting a single tweet (from the ID) is not limited in the same way as the search method – but the code does have a pause function to prevent the request being rejected by the Twitter site. The resulting spreadsheets were analysed in RStudio. The corpus is simply too large for Excel's limit (just over 1.08m. rows of data) at 1,353,460 rows. The next two major sections of the paper will discuss what was found in terms of the volume of tweets and the level of engagement with each Twitter.

Top top tweeters
This part of the paper will detail the overall demographics of the tweets gathered and will discuss the differences between each outlet's use of Twitter. The next table demonstrates the amount of followers, number of tweets since inception and when each respective media outlet joined the social media platform. What is obvious from the numbers is that the broadcasters have much higher follower counts than the newspapers: in the millions rather than the thousands. The BBC's position as trusted public broadcaster and Sky's historic relationship with sport, football and the English Premier League arguably exist outside of the political ideologies of the editorial stances of the newspapers. This, perhaps, gives them a much broader appeal at home and abroad. The Manchester United account is included as a comparison and to highlight the shifting media landscape in the coverage of sport. This type of sporting entity and their massive global reach mean that they are becoming media outlets in and of themselves. The Manchester United fan base is one of the largest in the world and its follower count is more than twice that of *BBC Sport*. As a result, the Manchester United feed has the ability to reach potentially more eyeballs than the journalism produced by the BBC. In purely news terms, this is narrowing the view of world sport to a single club and away from the more critical insights a journalist provides.

One interesting difference between each account is the inception dates and the disparities between when certain newspapers created a dedicated football channel. The *Sun* and *Mirror*, for example, created their football feeds years before their more general sport accounts. On the other hand, the all-sport content feeds of the

Jonathan Cable
Glyn Mottershead

Independent and *Telegraph* existed on Twitter years before they created football-focused accounts. This, perhaps, reflects their readership demographics and the continuing perception of football as a working class sport.

Outlet	Twitter Handle	Followers	Tweets Since Inception	Joined Twitter
BBC Sport	Bbcsport	7,170,000	316,000	March-11
Sky Sports News	Skysportsnews	5,800,000	68,700	January-10
ESPN FC	Espnfc	1,660,000	123,000	December-08
Guardian Sport	guardian_sport	766,000	155,000	June-09
Mirror Football	Mirrorfootball	490,000	342,000	October-08
Sun Football	Thesunfootball	373,000	145,000	February-09
Telegraph Football	Telefootball	290,000	84,800	November-13
Telegraph Sport	Telegraphsport	219,000	137,000	April-10
Sun Sport	Sunsport	149,000	83,200	December-11
Indy Football	Indyfootball	83,000	83,700	March-12
Metro Sport	metro_sport	71,500	63,400	April-10
Express Sport	dexpress_sport	53,400	104,000	May-10
Mirror Sport	Mirrorsport	34,200	54,700	January-10
Indy Sport	Indysport	31,600	83,300	October-08
Daily Mail Football	Mailfootball	30,600	57,400	May-10
In comparison:				
Man United	ManUtd	16,800,000	43,300	April-12

Table 2: Media outlets listed by number of followers (data accurate as of 14 January 2018)

The most prolific tweeters are the *BBC* and the *Mirror*, with the *Mirror*'s football account tweeting twice as much as most of the other accounts. Over time, however, there has been a collective increase in the sheer volume of tweets from these outlets. For instance, in 2011, all of these outlets produced just over 100,000 tweets, whereas in 2016 this number had increased to over 250,000. There are now many more people and outlets using Twitter and this has increased competition for attention. As a result, far more tweets are needed to be noticed. In addition, all content on an outlet's website is promoted on Twitter – not just select items.

Are you tweeting to me?
This section of the paper takes a closer look at the levels of interaction with the tweets from these outlets. Interaction with tweets represents an increased amount of emotional engagement with content. Even though it may seem like a small gesture to

retweet or 'favourite' content, it still takes a conscious decision to do so. The 'in reply' part of this section is concerned with which accounts media outlets are responding to or tweeting at. Examining this function of the Twitter feed helps uncover whether or not these accounts are using Twitter as a one- or two-way communication tool.

First the follower counts: what is plain to see is that the accounts with the larger follower counts have a greater engagement, apart from *Mirror Football* and *Guardian Sport* which have switched places. Where the differences arise is when the number of tweets with no engagement is considered. *Sky Sports News* only had 183 tweets with no retweet. This suggests that their content is attractive enough to users that they will happily retweet the vast majority of tweets.

Twitter Handle	Total Retweets	Tweets with no Retweets
bbcsport	11,449,413	1,930
skysportsnews	9,286,487	183
espnfc	4,899,689	8,668
mirrorfootball	2,805,117	34,677
guardian_sport	1,439,173	46,633
telefootball	1,160,156	2,297
thesunfootball	802,287	17,009
telegraphsport	416,016	16,160
metro_sport	368,992	10,972
indyfootball	319,241	24,290
sunsport	298,931	9,154
dexpress_sport	187,696	43,679
indysport	130,821	46,294
mirrorsport	149,969	26,423
mailfootball	45,748	38,842
Total	22,310,323	327,211

Table 3: Number of retweets per outlet (data accurate on 31 March 2017)

The following identifies the top five retweets from *BBC Sport*:

Tweet	Number of Retweets
Manchester United will appoint Jose Mourinho as their new manager, *BBC Sport* understands (*BBC Sport* 2016a)	12,771
For the next 10 days, Chelsea's Fernando Torres is a reigning World Cup, European Championship, Champions League & Europa League winner, #CFC (*BBC Sport* 2013a)	10,710

Jonathan Cable
Glyn Mottershead

David Beckham: 'I won't receive any salary during my time at Paris Saint-Germain, my salary will go to a children's charity in Paris', #PSG (*BBC Sport* 2013b)	10,589
Amazing scenes in the studio after #ENG's winner against #WAL! (*BBC Sport* 2016b)	10,312
What a fantastic gesture from the Dortmund fans (*BBC Sport* 2017)	8,518

Table 4: Top five retweets for *BBC Sport* Twitter feed

This helps illustrate the fact that the retweets are dominated by football. The *BBC Sport* feed, it must be noted, is about general sporting news but football is clearly the most popular. What is also evident is that these tweets are emotionally very positive in nature whether it is celebrating the successes of an athlete or praising a set of fans. The 'favourite' count is somewhat similar to the retweets but it is clear that fewer people are inclined to 'favourite' a tweet compared to retweeting:

Twitter Handle	Total Favourites	Tweets with no Favourite
bbcsport	10,104,480	12,951
skysportsnews	5,734,016	2,586
espnfc	4,904,065	16,532
mirrorfootball	1,216,454	78,398
guardian_sport	909,226	65,963
telefootball	850,443	3,171
thesunfootball	579,707	25,532
metro_sport	173,050	18,326
telegraphsport	217,414	30,944
indyfootball	197,035	27,461
dexpress_sport	114,615	48,216
sunsport	115,211	18,465
indysport	88,248	53,848
mailfootball	71,506	43,184
mirrorsport	70,089	28,041
Total	1,529,3075	473,618

Table 4: Number of 'favourites' per outlet (data accurate on 31 March 2017)

In contrast, the *Mirror Football* feed had the following top five 'favourites':

Tweet	Number of Favourites
Missing: 23-year-old French midfielder. Answers to Paul. Last seen dancing. If found, please call 1-800-JOSE (*Mirror Football* 2016a)	2,504
Paul Gascoigne reveals 14 lines of cocaine made him think killer Raoul Moat was his brother (*Mirror Football* 2015)	1,216
Richard Keys: 'I accept our prehistoric banter is not acceptable in a modern world' (*Mirror Football* 2011)	1,008
Four years after being diagnosed with leukaemia, Stan Petrov is set to return to training (*Mirror Football* 2016b)	981
BREAKING: Sunderland drop points against Man United (*Mirror Football* 2014)	796

PAPER

The difference to *BBC Sport* is clear with more a mix of positive and negative emotional sentiments. The football feed is playing more into fan rivalries and football culture by targeting certain clubs, players and events. But the numbers are still very small when compared to the total number of tweets sent out by *Mirror Football*. Finally for this section is 'in reply to', in other words 'direction interaction' with other Twitter users. Overall, this is very minimal. When an @ is included in a tweet it is usually self-referential of the outlet or writer of an article. For instance, *Mirror Football* tweeted @ its own name 2,443 times. These feeds are not used to interact with other uses. It is much less a social use of a digital platform and more of a broadcast, one-way conversation.

A game of words

This next section aims to highlight what these accounts are tweeting about. Looking at the hashtags used will show the key words targeted by these outlets to increase tweet engagement and appeal to a wider audience. The paper will then move on to discuss the most common pairs and triplets of words. From this the main topics mentioned will be identified. Firstly, it is abundantly clear that the Manchester United-related #MUFC is the most popular hashtag. Moreover, only three of the top 30 hashtags related to sport feature something other than football. The three non-football-related hashtags were #ashes, #bbccricket and #Wimbledon. And in the football category, it is the elite, extremely wealthy teams of the English Premier League which dominate with 16 out of the 30 most popular hashtags related to just this league.

It is also apparent that the accounts are used for self-referential attention, such as the previously mentioned #bbccricket or #ssn (which stands for *Sky Sports News*). The self-referential approach to the use of social media is not restricted to hashtags. In the various popular combinations of words found in the content we see that

Jonathan Cable
Glyn Mottershead 'via guardian' is the third most common pair of words, and 'espn soccer net' is the most popular triple word combination. When this is combined with the @ in reply results some of these media outlets appear to be merely talking to themselves.

As with the hashtags, football dominates these exchanges. Prominent football clubs, high profile managers and even scores appear regularly. Indeed, it is clear from the triple combination of words that Twitter is being used by the organisations like a broadcast tool. Terms such as 'you need to', 'need to know', 'things we learned' and 'follow it live' are all prominent and point towards the most popular content of match previews, match reports and live coverage. Added to this, there is football transfer news, often accompanied with tantalising headlines.

Conclusion

This paper demonstrates clearly that, as Twitter is increasingly adopted by media outlets, its usage is focused on providing an electronic funnel to an outlet's home website. This is at the expense of the social interaction aspects of Twitter. Moreover, it is in contrast to the comparable media of the live-blog, the use of which Thurman and Walters (2013) found to incorporate much higher levels of interactivity and connection with the audience. The key difference here is that perhaps it is a journalist who controls the live-blog while tweets on an official feed may be automated. That aside, the levels of retweets, 'favourites' and lack of @ replies demonstrate that Twitter is used by these official accounts as a traditional broadcast platform and not as a vehicle for encouraging conversations. In many ways this amounts to a severe undervaluing and underuse of the Twitter platform. If the competition is for eyeballs then surely the way to build a community and audience is to interact and not to churn out unsatisfying yet tasty morsels of clickbait for the audience to gorge themselves on.

References

Bakir, Vian and McStay, Andrew (2017) Fake news and the economy of emotions: Problems, causes, solutions, *Digital Journalism* pp 1-22. Available online at http://www.tandfonline.com/doi/full/10.1080/21670811.2017.1345645, accessed on 16 January 2018

BBC Sport (2013a) For the next 10 days, Chelsea's Fernando Torres is a reigning World Cup, European Championship, Champions League & Europa League winner, #CFC, *BBC Sport*. Available online at https://twitter.com/bbcsport/status/334779582945308673, accessed on 16 January 2018

BBC Sport (2013b) David Beckham: 'I won't receive any salary during my time at Paris Saint-Germain, my salary will go to a children's charity in Paris', #PSG, 31 January. Available online at https://twitter.com/bbcsport/status/297025294450184192, accessed on 16 January 2018

BBC Sport (2016a) Manchester United will appoint Jose Mourinho as their new manager, *BBC Sport* understands, 21 May. Available online at https://twitter.com/BBCSport/status/734110105499799552/photo/1, accessed on 16 January 2018

BBC Sport (2016b) Amazing scenes in the studio after #ENG's winner against #WAL!, 16 June. Available online at https://twitter.com/BBCSport/status/743474812924854272, accessed on 16 January 2018

BBC Sport (2017) What a fantastic gesture from the Dortmund fans, 11 April. Available online at https://twitter.com/bbcsport/status/851918799259533312?lang=en, accessed on 16 January 2018

Berger, Jonah and Milkman, Katherine L. (2012) What makes online content viral?, *Journal of Marketing Research*, Vol. 49, No. 2 pp 192-205

Blom, Jonas Nygaard and Hansen, Kenneth Reinecke (2015) Click bait: Forward-reference as lure in online news headlines, *Journal of Pragmatics*, Vol. 76 pp 87-100

Chen, Yimin et al. (2015) *Misleading online content: Recognizing clickbait as 'false news'*. Paper delivered at ACM workshop on multimodal deception detection, Seattle, Washington, USA, 9 November

Dick, Murray (2011) Search engine optimisation in UK news production, *Journalism Practice*, Vol. 5, No. 4 pp 462-477

Football365 (2017) Mediawatch. Available online at http://www.football365.com/features/mediawatch, accessed on 16 January 2018

Gill, Kieran et al. (2016) Premier League's big five clubs Manchester United, City, Chelsea, Arsenal and Liverpool hold secret meeting in London over Champions League format. *MailOnline*, 2 March. Available online at http://www.dailymail.co.uk/sport/sportsnews/article-3472523/England-s-big-five-clubs-Manchester-United-City-Chelsea-Arsenal-Liverpool-hold-secret-meeting-London-American-billionaire-European-Super-League.html, accessed on 16 January 2018

Guardian_Sport (2014) Five things we have learned from Manchester United's US tour, *Guardian_Sport*, 6 August. Available online at https://twitter.com/guardian_sport/status/496999598511366144, accessed on 16 January 2018

Iarovici, Edith and Amel, Rodica (1989) The strategy of the headline, *Semiotica*, Vol. 77, No. 4 pp 441-459

Kuiken, Jeffrey et al. (2017) Effective headlines of newspaper articles in a digital environment, *Digital Journalism* pp 1300-1314. Available online at http://www.tandfonline.com/doi/abs/10.1080/21670811.2017.1279978, accessed on 16 January 2018

Loewenstein, George (1994) The psychology of curiosity: A review and reinterpretation, *Psychological Bulletin*, Vol. 116, No. 1 pp 75-98

Mail Sport (2016) Man Utd, City, Chelsea, Arsenal & Liverpool chiefs in secret meeting over Euro Super League, 2 March. Available online at https://twitter.com/MailSport/status/704979582034771968, accessed on 16 January 2018

Merrington, Jacqui (2017) The shocking change that's turned the Cornwall newsroom digital (and why we don't do clickbait), *Cornwall Live*, 19 September. Available online at http://www.cornwalllive.com/news/news-opinion/shocking-change-thats-turned-cornwall-501664, accessed on 16 January 2018

Mirror Football (2011) Richard Keys: 'I accept our prehistoric banter is not acceptable in a modern world', 26 January. Available online at https://twitter.com/mirrorfootball/status/30259072452263937?lang=en, accessed on 16 January 2018

Mirror Football (2014) BREAKING: Sunderland drop points against Man United, 24 August. Available online at https://twitter.com/mirrorfootball/status/503585456945389569, accessed on 16 January 2018

Mirror Football (2015) Paul Gascoigne reveals 14 lines of cocaine made him think killer Raoul Moat was his brother, 30 November. Available online at https://twitter.com/mirrorfootball/status/671462953665851392, accessed on 16 January 2018

Mirror Football (2016a) Missing: 23-year-old French midfielder. Answers to Paul. Last seen dancing. If found, please call 1-800-JOSE, *Mirror Football*, Available online at https://twitter.com/mirrorfootball/status/774583576092368896, accessed on 16 January 2018

Jonathan Cable
Glyn Mottershead

Mirror Football (2016b) Four years after being diagnosed with leukaemia, Stan Petrov is set to return to training, 23 June. Available online at https://twitter.com/MirrorFootball/status/745940726354165760, accessed on 16 January 2018

Silverman, Craig (2015) Lies, damn lies and viral content, *Tow Center for Digital Journalism*. Available online at http://towcenter.org/wp-content/uploads/2015/02/LiesDamnLies_Silverman_TowCenter.pdf, accessed on 16 January 2018

Thurman, Neil and Walters, Anna (2013) Live blogging: Digital journalism's pivotal platform? A case study of the production, consumption and form of live blogs at *Guardian.co.uk*, *Digital Journalism*, Vol. 1, No. 1 pp 82-101

Wahl-Jorgensen, Karin (2013) *Emotional architecture of social media: The Facebook 'like' button*. Paper presented at the 63rd annual conference of the International Communication Association (ICA), London, 17-21 June

Note on the contributors

Jonathan Cable is a Lecturer in Sport Journalism at the University of Gloucestershire. He joined them from Cardiff University where he was a lecturer and researcher. He attained his PhD in Journalism Studies from Cardiff University in 2012. His research interests lie in football culture, protest, and sport media. His first book, *Protest campaigns, media and political opportunities*, has just been published.

Glyn Mottershead is a former regional newspaper journalist with more than 20 years in journalism and journalism training. He is co-director of the MSc in Computational and Data Journalism at Cardiff University and a co-author of the *21st century journalism handbook*. His work involves teaching people that numbers and data sets are not anywhere near as scary as they might first appear.

Charles M. Lambert

How to get kicked off Twitter: An examination of the changing ethics of the so-called 'tech giants'

This paper aims to contribute to the growing field of research into the ethical codes of social media and other 'big tech' companies by analysing two instances where internationally regarded journalists were suspended or removed from web-based media platforms. It will argue that the current focus on tech companies' responsibilities to protect users has led them to place less emphasis on freedom of speech than they did previously.

Key words: Andrew Jennings, Automattic, cricket, ethics, social media, Twitter, Wordpress

Introduction
The speed with which social media expanded left little time for ethical reflection. Facebook (FB), for example, was only made available outside educational institutions in 2006 and, by 2012, boasted more than one billion active users (Facebook 2018).

There has been a significant amount of research into the ethics of using social media from the point of view of practitioners (e. g., Couldry 2012, Lipschultz 2018). Increasingly, this is being supplemented by research into the approaches of the social media companies themselves. Bulut (2016), for example, studied the 2013 Gezi Park protests in Istanbul, Turkey, and argues that 'FB and Twitter have chosen to act in accordance with national policies even though Twitter is slightly more resistant to cooperation'. During the 2016 US Presidential election. Lori Bergen, president of the Association for Education in Journalism and Mass Communication, called on social media platforms 'to ensure ethical transparency in curating and disseminating news' (AEJMC 2016).

The paper was conceived at a time when there was widespread criticism of social media and technology companies for failing to monitor or restrain users of or contributors to their platforms.

Charles M.
Lambert

For example, ahead of the 2017 Conservative Party Conference, UK foreign secretary Boris Johnson was interviewed by the *Sun* newspaper. He said: 'They [the "tech giants"] don't pay any tax. They are facilitating terror. It is unbelievable. They need to be punished. ... They justify it on free speech and all this kind of stuff – but it's just money-making' (Newton Dunn 2017). Two months later, a leading British Labour MP, Yvette Cooper, the chair of the home affairs select committee, accused YouTube of continuing to host a propaganda video from a banned far right group, National Action, eight months after she had first drawn attention to it (Home affairs committee 2017). She also accused Twitter of failing to take down 'violent threats towards the current Prime Minister and a former Prime Minister, and again very racist abuse towards [Labour politician] Diane Abbott' after they had been reported. At an earlier hearing of the committee, another Labour MP, David Winnick, had accused Facebook, Google and Twitter of 'commercial prostitution' (Travis 2017).

The criticism, from left and right, that tech companies are too *laissez-faire* in their handling of material posted on their platforms masks the fact that, on occasion, these organisations can move swiftly and without warning to sanction users, including investigative journalists. Some social media users *do* find their accounts suspended or closed, in some cases within hours of posting. The 2016 Olympics provide a good example of this when, under pressure from the International Olympic Committee (IOC), social media companies were quick to delete posts that appeared to infringe copyright. A Venezuelan Twitter user with more than 40,000 followers, Luigino Bracci Roa, claimed his account was permanently closed after he posted seven videos of Olympic events, all of them less than 90 seconds in length (Moody 2016). According to *Buzzfeed News*, this was not an isolated case, with Twitter taking down clips that appeared to breach IOC copyright 'within minutes' (Warren 2016).

Twitter has also penalised users for breach of privacy. The *Independent*'s Los Angeles correspondent Guy Adams criticised NBC's decision to delay the transmission of the opening ceremony of the 2012 Olympic Games and published the email address of the president of NBC Olympics. The email address in question was a work email, not a private one. However, NBC complained and Adams's account was, briefly, suspended. Twitter later conceded: 'We did mess up' (Rogers 2012). Indeed, as Rossalyn Warren highlights (2016), there is a stark disparity between the way Twitter, in particular, deals with complaints by individuals who feel they have been abused or harassed compared to how it handles companies' complaints about copyright infringements.

This paper attempts to understand the ethical perspective which underpins this disparity and to contribute to the wider debate about social media ethics. It examines two instances where tech companies closed or suspended the accounts of sports journalists. The case studies have been chosen because, in both cases, the journalists are well-known, in Britain and further afield, having worked for mainstream media as well as carrying out citizen journalism. Moreover, the accounts in question were important tools, central to their journalism. Both authors were interviewed for this paper, though, in the case of Nishant Joshi, the research draws mainly on a podcast he posted on the audio-sharing site *Soundcloud* shortly after his Twitter account was suspended (*Radio Cricket* 2017).

Throughout the paper, the terms 'tech giant' or 'tech company' are used. They have become common in the British media as catch-all terms to refer to Alphabet (owners of Google), Facebook, Twitter, Automattic (owners of Wordpress), Verizon (owner of AOL and Yahoo) and other organisations involved in web-based communication. The term, while imprecise, is preferred to 'social media company' as several are not solely concerned with social networks, as defined by Lipschultz (2018: 353) as a platform that enables communication between site accounts.

Case study one: @altcricket
Nishant Joshi has a full-time job as a doctor in critical care and his cricket journalism is a sideline. While training in medicine in the Czech Republic, he published an anthology of cricket writing, the *Alternative cricket almanac* (2011), which showcased largely unknown bloggers, many of whom went on to become established cricket writers. A Twitter account, set up to promote the book, @altcricket, helped raise his profile to the point when he was invited to be a pundit on India's *Star Sports*. He has also raised money to help develop cricket in Afghanistan and for an orphanage in Africa.

Joshi built up almost 100,000 followers for his @altcricket Twitter account and, in particular, it enabled him to make contact with James Marsh, who became his co-presenter on a podcast called *Radio Cricket*. He also used it to make contacts with cricketers such as Dale Steyn, the South African fast bowler who was a guest on the 100th edition of *Radio Cricket* (*Radio Cricket* 2015). It has been a key tool in his efforts to raise money; he used it to help the charity, Cricket without Boundaries, raise £200,000 by playing the highest ever game of cricket on Mount Kilimanjaro.

British-based Joshi often appears bemused by the way that Indian cricket fans treat the leading players like demi-gods and he seems to enjoy poking fun at this intense adoration. For example, in the introduction to the previously mentioned 100th edition, he says:

Charles M.
Lambert

... yes, that is episode 100, the same number of international centuries that Sachin Tendulkar scored. It's taken us four years to reach this landmark which is apparently about the same time that it took between Sachin's 99th and 100th centuries (ibid). (In fact, Tendulkar needed 34 innings after his 99th century to reach his 100th – a period of around two and a half months.)

When, however, in March 2017, he joked about another Indian batsman, it provoked a fierce backlash and his Twitter account was abruptly suspended. Virat Kohli, the India cricket captain and arguably the best batsman in the world at the time, was injured and, as a result, was not playing in the fourth and final Test of India's series against Australia. However, during the drinks break, he did come on, carrying water for his team mates. Many of his fans – and, indeed, professional journalists – were tweeting or commenting on his amazing humility for being prepared to carry the drinks for his team mates. For example, the YouTube channel of Xtra Time.in posted pictures of Kohli with the drinks tray under the heading: 'Must watch! Virat Kohli carries drinks during break.'

> Indian captain Virat Kohli once again proved he is a perfect team-man. Kohli, who is not playing in Dharamsala, was seen carrying drinks for his team-mates during the first session of the Test Match. The Indian captain was seen trotting out onto the field with drinks, which became viral on social media. The commentators were also taken aback by such a move from Virat (Xtra Time 2017).

Joshi argues that this tweet was a comment on the extreme nature of his fans rather than on Kohli himself: the man carrying the drinks tray attracted more attention than those on the field of play in a deciding Test. 'You had hordes and hordes of blind-worshippers throwing themselves at the feet of Virat Kohli' (*Radio Cricket* 2017).

He responded with a tweet which read: 'Kohli scores century: HE'S THE GREATEST. Kohli scores duck: HE'S STILL THE GREATEST. Kohli carries drinks: WITNESS THE HUMILITY OF GOD (cited by Talwar 2017).

Although Twitter have not, to my knowledge, commented publicly on the suspension, Joshi believes it was this tweet which led to @ altcricket being closed. 'I think it got to a Kohli fan club and then another Kohli fan club and it spread like a virus ... then some Kohli fan account said: "Let's try and get him banned. Let's get him banned." I woke up the next day to get a message saying my account had been suspended' (*Radio Cricket* 2017).

Unlike Guy Adams (above), Joshi was not able to appeal against the suspension because he no longer had access to the email account which was linked to @altcricket. (Twitter now regularly asks users to confirm that their email address is still current – presumably to deal with this issue.) The offending tweet was widely retweeted but the retweets do not appear to have been removed from the micro-blogging site. Twitter's terms of service state that 'you understand that by using the services, you may be exposed to content that might be offensive, harmful, inaccurate or otherwise inappropriate' (Twitter 2018).

It is a sign of the importance attached to social media that the news of Joshi's suspension was picked up by the Indian edition of the *Daily Mail* (Dawkins 2017). The writer of the article approached Twitter for comment but had not received one by the time it was published. I have also approached Twitter and not received a reply.

Case Study Two: *Transparency in Sport*

Investigative journalist Andrew Jennings is the author of several books, the best known being *The new lords of the rings: Olympic corruption and how to buy gold medals* (1996) about the International Olympic Committee, and *Foul!* (2006) which investigated FIFA, the international football association. He is the presenter of several documentaries for ITV and BBC *Panorama* programmes about corruption in football, most notably *FIFA's dirty secrets* (broadcast on 29 November 2010) which is credited with helping bring about the downfall of former FIFA president Sepp Blatter. He is a regular conference contributor on both sides of the Atlantic.

In September 2013, he noticed that his Wordpress.com site, *Transparency in Sport*, had disappeared. He looked into it and it turned out – according to 'Phil' who was, apparently, a Wordpress 'trust and safety adviser', that the site had been taken down following a complaint from a Russian law firm. And this is the complaint (with grammatical errors throughout):

> Myself, Robert William, CEO and one of the editor in CrimeFashion. My website url is http://crimefashion.netne.net. I posted a lot of news from all around the world. And my site reaches to lot of peoples and we have a very good customers. Two days before we saw that some person who is using wordpress blog is copyied [sic] some content from our site and posted in his blogs. It is illegal. And we are the copyright owners of that content, others don't have the rights to copy my content. So please check that two links and please remove it as soon as possible (Jennings 2014).

Jennings contacted Wordpress's lawyers; he also contacted their PR company in New York. 'I spent quite a bit of time pointing out that I was known, that I worked for American universities as well as British ones' (Jennings 2017). But in the end he gave up. 'It was time to move on. I wanted Blatter,' he said (ibid).

It's not clear whether or not the account has now been reinstated. Visitors to *TransparencyInSportBlog.Wordpress.com* will see a message saying that to view the site you need a wordpress.com account and permission from Jennings. By the time I interviewed Jennings for this paper, he could no longer remember his password. So the site is effectively dead though most of the content has been archived elsewhere. The website *http://crimefashion.netne.net* no longer exists; it may never have done. In any event, it would probably not have been difficult for Wordpress to have investigated whether or not Jennings had plagiarised material from this site.

Automattic, the owner of *wordpress.com*, prides itself on managing millions of blogs with relatively few employees. Its website includes a chart, titled 'One of these things is not like the other' which shows that it has 164 million unique views per month, yet only employs 670 people. This is far fewer employees than Google (72,053), Facebook (20,658) or Twitter (3,583) (Automattic 2018). This, perhaps, explains why the company is reluctant to investigate complaints.

America's Digital Millennium Copyright Act (DMCA) exempts online service providers (OSPs) from copyright law so long as they comply with the terms of the Act. One of conditions is that 'when given a proper notice of infringing material being posted on its network', the OSP 'responds expeditiously to remove, or disable access to, the material that is claimed to be infringing' (Pike & Fischer Inc. 2003: 30). The Act allows the original publisher to demonstrate that their content does not include 'infringing material' but Jennings was reluctant to put his private details in the public domain:

> Under DCMA they claim they have to pass on any details. 'You've got to send us your details.' I said: 'I'm not going to send my details to people who are going to harm me' (Jennings 2017).

Andrew Jennings is an award-winning investigative journalist; there are people who regard him as their enemy; he doesn't want to reveal a lot of personal details and he certainly can't reveal the source of all the content on his site.

Regular users of social media, particularly Twitter, will be accustomed to seeing notices reporting that tweets have been removed under the provisions of the DCMA. The effects of the Act are discussed below. Automattic were approached for comment on the suspension of Jennings' site but have not responded.

Conclusion: Changing ethics in social media

In both the case studies examined above, a journalist's account with a major tech company has been abruptly closed in response to a complaint or complaints. In both cases, these accounts are important to their work as journalists. And, in both cases, there do not appear to have been any attempts by the tech company to investigate the validity of the complaints.

In Nishant Joshi's case, there are no claims being made in the tweet, so there is no issue of libel; there is no copyrighted material being shared; there are no offensive phrases being used and no threats of violence. Joshi describes himself as 'a Kohli fan' (*Radio Cricket* 2017) and insists his criticism was aimed at supporters and the media rather than the player himself. In any case, professional sports men and women face far worse abuse on Twitter on a daily basis.

The issue in this case (though without any official comment from Twitter, this cannot be confirmed) appears to be the sheer number of complaints – almost certainly running into the thousands. While the tweet itself does not appear exceptional, it would appear that, at some point, the sheer weight of numbers drew it to the attention of Twitter's censors. They, in turn, would have noticed that many of the complaints were orchestrated by a small handful of individual users which may have made them cautious about taking further action. This raises a concern as to whether insulting someone who is immensely popular or well-known should be should treated differently to an attack on someone who is less famous.

The case also raises issues of commercial interest. Lipschultz (2018: 272), in his discussion of social media ethics, remarks that 'editorial independence may be compromised when special interests override larger public interests'. In this case, cricket is one of the most discussed topics on Twitter in India, which has the world's second largest population. So the potential damage caused by alienating cricket fans in India is considerably greater than that caused by upsetting one journalist. Clearly the continued participation of some high-profile figures on Twitter is vital to the company's business – not least President Donald Trump. Stock market analyst James Cakmak has estimated that were Trump to leave Twitter (or be suspended), it would wipe $2 billion in market value off the company (Bloomberg 2017).

Andrew Jennings's case would, on the surface, seem to have been easy to investigate, simply by checking whether or not the Robert William of *http://crimefashion.netne.net* actually exists. Instead, the company simply followed its obligations under the DMCA. This, in turn, had the effect of placing the onus on Jennings to prove he had *not* breached William's copyright rather than on William (or

Charles M.
Lambert

the firm that brought the complaint using that name) to prove he *had* done so.

Big tech companies have, however, been reluctant to conduct investigations. The pioneers of silicon valley insisted that they simply wanted to enable communication, they did not seek power over it. This is evidenced in both the companies' codes of conduct and their public pronouncements:

- Twitter's terms of service state that users retain their rights to any content they submit, post or display on or through the service. 'We may not monitor or control the content posted via the services and we cannot take responsibility for such content' (Twitter 2018).

- Wordpress says: 'We host millions of web sites for our users and are not able to control or police the hundreds of thousands of blog posts our users create every day' (Automattic 2018).

- In August 2016, Mark Zuckerberg, Facebook founder and chief executive officer, said: 'We're proud of being a tech company and not a media company … we build the tools, we do not produce any content. … The world needs news companies, but also technology platforms, like what we do, and we take our role in this very seriously' (Segreti 2016).

- In a case involving a former Conservative council candidate who unsuccessfully sued Google for libel over comments published by a third party on its Blogger platform, Google argued that it could not be regarded as a *publisher* (Kiss and Arthur 2013).

Even when offensive, misleading, invasive or illegal content was posted on these sites, the companies relied on users to raise them. The idea of proactively policing their pages appeared neither desirable nor, given the sheer amount of content involved, practicable. This attitude is summed up eloquently in an editorial in the *Spectator* magazine:

> Companies such as Google and Facebook insist they're the digital equivalent of the vans, newsagents and paperboys who distribute what other people publish. So they ought not be held responsible for it (*Spectator* 2017).

One might extend this simile to say that just as the newsagents, van rental companies and paperboys were free to decide to terminate their business or employment with a particular newspaper group without giving any reason, so Twitter or Wordpress are free to suspend their relationships with journalists such as Joshi or Jennings.

But this is where the comparison breaks down. While a newspaper could switch its custom to a different van company, Nishant Joshi cannot switch to a different micro-blogging social media site –

because Dale Steyn and his other valuable contacts use Twitter. Journalists are locked into the big social media companies in the same way as we were once locked into using the telephone. The *Spectator* goes on to argue that the 'we're platforms, not publishers', argument changed with the advent of social media:

> The tech giants, worried by the demons they were nurturing, started to behave as publishers. They began moderating and sometimes banning content. Facebook started to editorialise its news feed, tweaking 'emotional content' to see if it would make users happy or sad. They stopped being mere platforms (ibid).

It would seem that, tacitly if not publicly, the tech giants have come to realise this. The most obvious example of this being Facebook's decision, in May 2017, to hire an extra 3,000 editors to screen posts. We may well see other companies following suit, albeit on a smaller scale. At the UK home affairs select committee meeting, referred to at the start of this paper, representatives of Google and Facebook also both said they were now proactively seeking out content that violated their polices rather than depending on it being reported to them. '99 per cent of the content we take down involving ISIS and al-Qaeda comes through our own efforts of finding that content rather than content reported to us,' Simon Milner, Facebook's UK policy director, stated (Home affairs committee 2017).

Perhaps most surprising was the response from Twitter, which once declared itself 'the free-speech wing of the free-speech party' (Halliday 2012). Sinead McSweeney, the European and African vice-president of public policy and communications for Twitter, said that safety was its 'number one priority' in 2017. She added: 'You cannot be on our platform if you are affiliated with a group that encourages violence against protected groups' (Home affairs committee 2017).

It is understandable that the committee members were concerned with the suppression of offensive or terrorist material. Several MPs have received death threats and the United Kingdom was subjected to at least five terrorist attacks in 2017, with social media seen as a recruiting sergeant for the attackers (ibid). Yet, there was not one question to the tech companies' representatives about whether, on occasion, they could be too quick to endorse complaints, nor any concern expressed about the impact that their more proactive policing regimes might have on freedom of expression.

In 2014, business analyst Brian Solis wrote:

> The ethical practice of social media starts with an ethical foundation. Without it, you risk falling victim to social media's relentless and unforgiving nature of real-time relevance or irrelevance. … Without a strong ethical foundation, you

Charles M. Lambert

unintentionally make perilous decisions driven by what's right ... right now, rather than what's truly right (Solis 2014: xvi).

While Solis's advice was directed at *users* of social networks, it could equally be applied to the companies that have established them. The tech giants are now behaving as both publishers and regulators and, as such, wield greater potential influence than any newspaper or television company has ever enjoyed in a liberal democracy. It is to be hoped that lawmakers consider how to protect free comment in their future dealings with these companies.

References

AEJMC (2016) Journalism educators urge social media platforms to ensure ethical transparency in curating and disseminating news. Available online at http://www.aejmc.org/home/2016/06/pac-060316/, accessed on 16 January 2018

Automattic (2018) About us. Available online at https://automattic.com/about/, accessed on 16 January 2018

Bloomberg (2017) Here's how valuable Trump is to Twitter (video). Available online at https://www.bloomberg.com/news/articles/2017-08-17/what-is-trump-worth-to-twitter-one-analyst-estimates-2-billion, accessed on 16 January 2018

Bulut, Ergin (2016) Social media and the nation state: Of revolution and collaboration, *Media, Culture & Society*, Vol. 38, No. 4, May. Available online at http://journals.sagepub.com/doi/abs/10.1177/0163443716643013, accessed on 16 January 2018

Couldry, Nick (2012) *Media, society, world: Social theory and digital media practice*, Cambridge, Polity Press

Dawkins, David (2017) 'Tendulkar, burning!' Twitter and the war against criticism in India, *MailOnline India*, 31 March. Available online at http://www.dailymail.co.uk/indiahome/indianews/article-4369614/Cricket-blogger-s-Twitter-suspension-sparks-debate.html, accessed on 16 January 2018

DiStaso, Marcia W. and Bortree, Denise Sevick (eds) *The ethical practice of social media in public relations*, Abingdon, Oxon, Routledge

Halliday, Josh (2012) Twitter's Tony Wang: 'We are the free speech wing of the free speech party', *Guardian*, 22 March. Available online at https://www.theguardian.com/media/2012/mar/22/twitter-tony-wang-free-speech, accessed on 16 January 2018

Home affairs committee (2017) *Oral evidence: Hate crime and its violent consequences, HC* 683. Available online at http://data.parliament.uk/writtenevidence/committeeevidence.svc/evidencedocument/home-affairs-committee/hate-crime-and-its-violent-consequences/oral/75919.html, accessed on 16 January 2018

Jennings, Andrew (2014) Attention WordPress gathering this weekend in San Francisco: Which one of you destroyed my journalism?, Twitter, 24 October. Available online at https://twitter.com/AAndrewJennings/status/525791044257193984, accessed on 16 January 2018

Jennings, Andrew (2017) Interview with the author, 20 October 2017

Kiss, Jemima and Arthur, Charles (2013) Publishers or platforms? Media giants may be forced to choose, *Guardian*, 29 July. Available online at https://www.theguardian.com/technology/2013/jul/29/twitter-urged-responsible-online-abuse, accessed on 16 January 2018

Lipschulz, Jeremy Harris (2018) *Social media communication: Concepts, practices, data, law and ethics*, New York, Routledge, second edition

Moody, Glyn (2016) Total tweet delete: Olympics fan claims Twitter killed his account after he posted Rio videos, *Ars Technica*, 8 September. Available online at https://arstechnica.com/tech-policy/2016/08/olympics-fan-claims-twitter-killed-account-rio-videos/, accessed on 16 January 2018

Newton Dunn, Tom (2017) HIT TERROR TECH: Boris Johnson demands punishment for web giants like Amazon and YouTube for 'helping' terrorists, *Sun*, 29 September. Available online at https://www.thesun.co.uk/news/4580628/boris-johnson-punishment-amazon-youtube-terror/, accessed on 16 January 2018

Pike and Fisher Inc. (2003) *The Digital Millennium Copyright Act: Text, history, and case law*, Bethesda, Pike and Fischer

Radio Cricket (2015) 100: Dale Steyn. Available online at https://soundcloud.com/radiocricket/100-dale-steyn, accessed on 16 January 2018

Radio Cricket (2017) 130: What happened to AltCricket? The inside story. Available online at https://soundcloud.com/radiocricket/130-what-happened-to, accessed on 16 January 2018

Rogers, Katie (2012) Twitter 'sorry' for suspending Guy Adams as NBC withdraws complaint, *Guardian*, 31 July. Available online at https://www.theguardian.com/technology/2012/jul/31/guy-adams-twitter-growing-pains, accessed on 16 January 2018

Segreti, Giulia (2016) Facebook CEO says group will not become a media company, *Reuters*, 29 August. Available online at https://uk.reuters.com/article/us-facebook-zuckerberg/facebook-ceo-says-group-will-not-become-a-media-company-idUKKCN1141WNL, accessed on 16 January 2018

Solis, Brian (2014) Foreword: Social media is lost without a social compass, DiStaso, Marcia W. and Bortree, Denise Sevick (eds) *The ethical practice of social media in public relations*, Abingdon, Routledge pp xv-xxiv

Spectator (2017) The tech giants have become publishing tycoons. Let's have laws to deal with them, *Spectator*, 14 October 2017 p. 3

Talwar, K. (2017) So this is why @AltCricket has been suspended. Indian cricket fans are Grade A arsehats, Twitter. Available online at https://twitter.com/search?q=%40BollywoodGandu%20%40altcricket&src=typd, accessed on 16 January 2018

Travis, Alan (2017) Face-off between MPs and social media giants over online hate speech, *Guardian*, 14 March. Available online at https://www.theguardian.com/media/2017/mar/14/face-off-mps-and-social-media-giants-online-hate-speech-facebook-twitter, accessed on 16 January 2018

Twitter (2018) Twitter terms of service. Available online at https://twitter.com/en/tos, accessed on 16 January 2018

Warren, Rossalyn (2016) Why isn't Twitter taking down harassment as fast as it takes down Olympics content?, *Buzzfeed*, 16 August. Available online at https://www.buzzfeed.com/rossalynwarren/i-cant-believe-they-deleted-that-perfect-santana-tweet?utm_term=.earzaQLDE2#.uqm6jVXDGz, accessed on 16 January 2018

Xtra Time (2017) Must Watch! Virat Kohli carries drinks during break, YouTube, Available online at https://www.youtube.com/watch?v=oNg2avYwgr4, accessed on 16 January 2018

Note on the contributor

Charles M. Lambert is Head of the Journalism and Media cluster at the University for the Creative Arts, in Farnham, Surrey. He spent two decades as a television journalist, covering news and sport for the BBC and ITV before becoming leader of the Sports Journalism degree course at the University of East London. His first book, *Digital sports journalism*, is due to be published later this year by Routledge. He has taught Philosophy and Ethics to A level students.

Anne Surma
Kristin Demetrious

Plastic words, public relations and the neoliberal transformation of twentieth century discourse

This paper argues that public relations and its relationship to communicative ethics played an integral, though hitherto under-theorised, political and cultural role in shaping the emergence and development of the neoliberal project in the twentieth century. Drawing on primary archival documents and synthesising a range of secondary material, the paper explores the proposition that public relations activities were instrumental in embedding the discursive and rhetorical impetus of ideas of freedom, the free market and free enterprise promoted by neoliberals in the USA during the 1930s–1940s, and that the cultural field linking to public relations was much more fertile than previously understood. The reach and diversity of twentieth-century public relations supporting the neoliberal agenda is not yet fully acknowledged. This has implications for our understanding of how public opinion is shaped in contemporary society and the ethical conduct of public debates pivotal to the phenomenon of neoliberalism.

Key words: discourse, neoliberalism, plastic words, propaganda, US public relations

'You must never slap a king – you have to kill him'
In the now vast body of literature on the rise of neoliberalism as economic theory, ideology and discursive and material practice, scholars have drawn attention to the role played by public relations (for example, Phelan 2014; Sriramesh and Vercic 2012; Steger and Roy 2010). However, public relations' active part in propagating the reach and impact of neoliberalism – whether explicitly *as* public relations or, indirectly, via print and broadcast journalism and popular entertainment; promotion and publicity on behalf of big business and private enterprise; school, university and community curricula; or through informal interpersonal networks and connections – has yet to be comprehensively and forensically investigated.[1]

In this paper, we examine specific ways in which public relations activities influenced the public about the ideas and ideals of neoliberalism during the 1930s and 1940s in the USA. The urgency motivating these activities stemmed from influential institutions, associations and individuals' vigorous response to the political and social context of the Great Depression of the 1930s and leading up to the Second World War. Arguably, one of the most crucial contributions that public relations endeavours made during this period in support of this response was through invoking and embedding the discourse of so-called free-market economics (specifically, 'free enterprise' or 'private enterprise') in the cultural imagination. This was achieved through rhetoric that, on the one hand, foretold the certain doom of remaining enthralled by the economic, civic, employment and infrastructure programme launched by President Franklin Delano Roosevelt's administration in 1933 and that, on the other, sketched an optimistic, if nebulously defined, future in which private enterprise and free individuals flourished unrestricted by government intervention and regulation. These communicative activities, we argue, were integral to laying the solid foundations that supported the rise of the neoliberal project in the US and internationally from the late 1940s onwards.

PAPER

Highlighting the selected communicative work of one US-based practitioner, James P Selvage (1902–1975), whose networks, relationships and activities in public relations were tied up with his dedication to the cause of private enterprise, we aim to offer a glimpse into the specific ways in which public relations has been engaged in the development and rise of the so-called neoliberal 'thought collective' that burgeoned from the late 1940s. Collating and synthesising a range of extant secondary material and drawing on primary archival documents, we suggest that, while certainly not monolithic or centrally co-ordinated, a concerted and sustained (individual, institutional, and corporate) public relations effort in the USA between the 1930s and 1940s was instrumental in communicating and embedding the discursive and rhetorical 'truth' of neoliberal economics and the 'freedoms' which it claimed to enable: the free individual, the free market, and free enterprise.

It is thus by means of illustration that we show that Selvage's particular assignments offer a salutary example of how public relations assisted in this achievement in three key ways. Firstly, this was through his involvement in powerful networks and relationships, including with corporations and corporate owners, professional associations, print and broadcast media, which exercised a dynamic influence on the lay public. Secondly, this was through the unabashed marshalling of public relations as the voice of business, the free market and free enterprise. And, finally, it was through the strategic use of language and what Uwe Poerksen (1995) calls 'plastic words' which bolstered the rhetorical

Anne Surma
Kristin
Demetrious

and discursive impetus of the domains of knowledge central to constructing and communicating the neoliberal project.

In the course of discussion, then, we show that public relations work over this period was pivotal to laying the strong foundations of a communicative network of individual, corporate, think-tank, government and educational interests sympathetic to the neoliberal ideology introduced into the US by thinkers and economists, including Ludwig von Mises and Friedrich Hayek, the economists at the centre of the neoliberal thought collective. This raises questions of how industry advocacy, working outside the explicit remit of public relations, for example in partnership with educational institutions and think tanks, may have become infused with political discourse in support of neoliberalism.

'The time has come to step in again': The emergence of neoliberal thought

Neoliberalism

Neoliberalism as an economic theory can only be fully appreciated by understanding its contradictions. Philip Mirowski remarks that 'a primary ambition of the neoliberal project is to *redefine the shape and functions of the state, not to destroy it*' (Mirowski 2015: 436; emphasis in original). Moreover, while neoliberals are sceptical about 'the lack of control of democracy', they understand that there does need to be 'a reliable source of popular legitimacy for the neoliberal market state'. Thus, they seek to overcome such an *'intolerable contradiction by treating politics as if it were a market and promoting an economic theory of democracy'* (ibid; emphasis in original). Implicit in Mirowski's references to the requirement to redefine the state and to promote an alternative version of democracy is the central role of communication in achieving these ambitions.

The discursive relationship and cultural field linking neoliberalism to the amalgam of communicative practices identifiable as public relations is wider and more fertile than previously understood and, as a consequence, we argue, more significant. However, that neoliberalism is a shifting, ill-defined concept has added to the challenge of understanding this relationship. As many have pointed out, neoliberalism has become a catch-all phrase that cannot do justice to the panoply of (often contradictory) free-market economic theories, principles and practices, philosophical beliefs and values spawned by its originators and supporters, as the seeds of the movement emerged, spreading from Europe (Austria, France, Germany, Switzerland) in the 1920s and 1930s, to the UK, the USA from the 1930s and 1940s, to become a global phenomenon from the 1980s onwards.

Daniel Stedman Jones refers to the period we consider in this paper as the first phase of neoliberalism (Stedman Jones 2012: 6). Our focus is specifically on the communicative commitment to the protection and growth of private enterprise, and on those who vehemently opposed what they regarded as socialist incursions by the state. As Angus Burgin points out:

> In the midst of the Great Depression, market advocates were acutely aware that the social philosophy of the free market inspired little support within either academic institutions or popular politics. They sought to overcome their isolation by establishing networks of sympathizers who could work in conjunction to reexamine the philosophical foundations of their ideas and reconstruct the public presentation of their arguments (Burgin 2012: 8).

The term 'neoliberal' was taken on by the participants in the Colloque Walter Lippmann, in Paris in 1938, a meeting dedicated to consider Lippmann's book of 1937, *The good society* (2017 [1937]),[2] which argues that a 'collectivist' approach to government is a step along the road to totalitarianism. The men who participated in this meeting would later form the core of the group that became the Mont Pèlerin society less than a decade later (Stedman Jones 2012: 6), the nucleus and starting point of 'primarily … a historical "thought collective" of increasingly global proportions' (Plehwe 2015: 4). The 'invisible college' of the Mont Pèlerin Society, formed in 1947 by Hayek and others attached to the political philosophies of Austrian School economist von Mises, works as a 'Rosetta Stone' to understanding the network of ideas and communities that form the thought collective (Mirowski 2015: 429).[3] The purpose of the 'handpicked' and shadowy society was to exercise wide but discreet influence on public opinion in support of their remodeled ideas about free market capitalism (ibid: 430). This support would be garnered in a number of ways and in different settings and would be used effectively to oppose the growing and popular doctrines of Keynesian collectivism that had influenced popular policies, such as Roosevelt's New Deal.

As we will go on to show below, in collating just a small selection of the range of communicative initiatives mobilised to promote the interests of the free market and US private enterprise during the 1930s and 1940s, the rhetorical and discursive ground enabling the neoliberal thought collective to take root was effectively tilled during this period by an influential network of organisations and individuals.

Opposing the New Deal
In order to address the deleterious social and economic impacts of the Great Depression following the financial crash of 1929, the US

Anne Surma
Kristin
Demetrious

government led by President Roosevelt implemented big-spending reforms and programmes, known as the New Deal. These initiatives were promoted by massively resourced public communications, as Kevin Moloney notes: '... in 1936 the Roosevelt administration employed 146 full-time and 124 part-time publicity agents who issued 7 million copies of 48,000 press releases' (Moloney 2006: 43).

Deeming the government's intervention as constituting unwarranted interference and as 'attacking individualism and freedom' (Fones-Wolf 1994: 24), private business and corporate interests reacted vigorously, perhaps most explicitly through the employer organisation, the National Association of Manufacturers (NAM), whose programme of the 1930s is the best-known example of Depression-era corporate public relations. 'The campaign's principal tenet was that the profit motive was a vital part of American business, and therefore government regulation was damaging' (Miller 1999: 23-24). Performed with quasi-religious zeal, the NAM's work was, as Richard Tedlow describes it, a 'public relations crusade' against American unionisation in the 1930s (1976: 29). The scale of tactics and texts that were used to support the right-wing offensive against New Deal policies included the American Way campaign in 1936. This was designed

> to challenge the fundamental social assumptions of the New Deal and to project a picture of American business as a system that – through its normal routines – responds to and meets the concerns and aspiration of ordinary Americans. The key was to present a case for American business not from the customary vantage points of the stockholder, but from 'the mass man's point of view' (Ewen 1996: 304).

This NAM-led avalanche of industry spending (on lobbying, campaign finance, litigation, philanthropy and funding research) and promotion (through advertising, market research and opinion polls) of free market enterprise and anti-unionism continued into the 1940s (van Elteren 2011).

A key public figure with links to the NAM and, thus, to the realm of public relations was the politically conservative journalist and author of, among other texts, *Economics in one lesson* (1946), Henry Hazlitt. (Hazlitt would, in 1947, become a founding member of and then longstanding and active participant in the activities of the Mont Pèlerin Society.)[4] Hazlitt had become interested in Austrian economics in the second decade of the twentieth century (Hazlitt 1984: 2). After stints at *The Nation*, where he wrote against the New Deal and Roosevelt's interventionist policies, and then at the *American Mercury*, in 1934 he joined *The New York Times* where, during a period of more than ten years, his often daily editorials and review essays gave him the opportunity to write on a range of topics promoting the free market, the damage inflicted by unionism, the ineffectiveness of foreign aid, and so on (Rockwell 1995).[5] Hazlitt was well connected, not only to those like him who would become members of the thought collective, including Jasper Elliot Crane, the most powerful business sponsor and supporter of the Mont Pèlerin Society, but to other individuals who also held positions with access to the public and hence the opportunity to shape public opinion.

Indeed, Crane's active involvement in the US conservative movement and his role as a member and financial sponsor of the Mont Pèlerin Society meant that his influence was far-reaching. Vice-President of the DuPont Company, which had been 'one of the centers of opposition to the New Deal during the 1930s' (Phillips-Fein 2015: 283), Crane was clearly not alone in his desire to defeat and counter the popularity of Roosevelt's New Deal. However, he is perhaps distinguished in seeking a deeper and more authoritative intellectual framework to stem the rise of the political left. In strategising a long term 'battle for minds', as Kim Phillips-Fein explains, Crane was searching, in his words, for the 'New Testament of capitalism', the 'bible' of free-enterprise (Phillips-Fein 2015: 285).

Another public figure, who reviewed Hazlitt's work favourably in his column and who would later contribute articles to *The Freeman*, the magazine of which Hazlitt was editor in the early 1950s, was the commentator and broadcaster, George E. Sokolsky. A committed libertarian and well-known columnist and broadcaster, Sokolsky also completed extensive freelance work for NAM (for the American Way campaign), carrying out interviews and helping to produce dozens of radio broadcasts to defend private enterprise (Stole 2005: 165). He also undertook work for the public relations firm Hill & Knowlton, and he was particularly close to John W Hill who was himself a staunch supporter of private enterprise.[6] Sokolsky also carried out freelance work for Selvage's agency.

The various parts played by NAM, Hazlitt, Crane, Sokolsky, Hill and others during the 1930s and 1940s as harbingers for the neoliberal cause can be seen as preempting Hayek's identification of the pivotal role of intellectuals in this venture, who, he claimed, wielded power 'by shaping public opinion' in the contemporary context (1949: 371). In his 1949 paper 'The intellectuals and socialism', Hayek argued that it was crucial for the neoliberal cause to find intellectuals who believed in a free society and who would, therefore, influence the public accordingly. Hayek defined intellectuals very precisely, as 'secondhand dealers in ideas', and among their number he included 'journalists, teachers, ministers, lecturers, publicists, radio commentators, writers of fiction, cartoonists and artists' (1949:

Anne Surma

Kristin Demetrious

372) as well as experts in other fields, such as scientists and doctors who, because of their expertise, commanded respect even when they spoke about subjects outside their sphere of knowledge. As this brief overview has shown, the US secondhand dealers in ideas of the 1930s and 1940s had already been energetically engaged in promoting the market and freedom for some fifteen years before Hayek issued his rallying call to intellectuals to combat the socialists' 'courage to be Utopian' (1949: 384).

James P Selvage: Public relations, America and the 'spirit of free enterprise'

It is in the context outlined above that the public relations 'counsel' and one-time public relations director for NAM, James P. Selvage, carried out his work as a secondhand dealer in ideas. While not a member of the coterie of academics and thinkers who attended the Lippmann seminar, Selvage certainly appears to have broadly shared their neoliberal values and ideas. Moreover, he was familiar with Henry Hazlitt's work, was a friend of Sokolsky and was politically committed to challenging the Roosevelt administration. Selvage was also closely connected to the public relations fraternity in New York during this period, for example, attending, in 1938, the first meeting of the 'Wise Men' convened by Hill (of Hill & Knowlton) which was attended by a group of senior public relations personnel from the largest corporations and public relations agencies in the city (Henderson 2010: 357-358).[8]

Selvage's perhaps best known popular contribution to NAM's promotion of free-market ideas is for his association with the radio series the *American Family Robinson*, a drama first aired in 1934, which centred on the lives of the Robinson family in a small industrial city named Centerville. The programme set out to counter New Deal principles and 'to teach economic lessons and to argue that Roosevelt's social policies were utopian and disruptive' (Fones-Wolf 1999: 230). Elizabeth Fones-Wolf explains that, within six months of its launch, the programme was being broadcast by 207 stations and by the late 1930s almost 300 small non-network stations aired the programme. 'The NAM paid production costs and either local employers bought airtime or stations provided it for free' (Fones-Wolf 1999: 230).

Although continuing his association with NAM, Selvage went on to head the consultancy Selvage and Smith and, in 1941, joined by Morris Lee (from the NAM), the agency became Selvage and Lee. Selvage's political affiliations are further reflected in the fact that he served as assistant to the chairman of the Republican National Committee from 1943 to 1944 (Manning, Selvage and Lee 2017).

For public relations professionals like Selvage, then, working in the industry in the 1940s involved collaborating with like-minded colleagues and organisations to challenge and transform the prevailing view of business and free enterprise as evil and government as good. From Selvage's perspective, public relations had a pivotal role to play in this endeavour, as articulated in his presentation entitled 'A look ahead at public relations' (Selvage 1942) which he delivered to the Advertising Club of Worcester and Industrial Executives of Worcester, on 4 November 1942. Here, Selvage's view of the inextricability of public relations and free enterprise is crystallised. In addition, the rhetoric of freedom is harnessed strategically to reinforce the discursive, visionary potential of a market-based and market-driven society.

The text of this address demonstrates that Selvage's aim is to raise concern among his audience about what he sees as the oppressive hand of government, exercising its power even more forcefully during this period of the Second World War. He also refers to the threat posed by 'our opponents in economic philosophy' (1942: 3) and to misguided 'radicals' who bandy about 'that dangerous word "liberal"'(1942: 4), thereby distracting Americans from their proper, nationalistic focus on supporting and enabling the flourishing of 'free enterprise' and 'free men'.[9] Here, Selvage denigrates the concept of freedom's associations with Roosevelt's version of liberalism, repositioning it in direct relation to the market and individualism.

Sliding between the first-person singular and the first-person plural voice (of the rhetorically assertive individual identifying with his audience), Selvage conjures a vision of the role of public relations and its responsibility to sell its 'merchandise' – American free enterprise – following the end of the war. He imagines a post-war context in which free enterprise is reborn, liberated from its current strictures of government regulation and control. His masculinist, quasi-aggressive tone is unapologetic as he pronounces that 'we must assume that vice-president Wallace's dreamy economics of a quart of free milk for every African savage have been washed away; that hard-headed Yankee ingenuity and individualism – which will win this war – will be permitted to rebuild after the peace' (1942: 1). In a direct rebuttal of Vice-President Wallace's speech, 'The century of the common man' delivered in New York some months previously, in May 1942 (Wallace 1942),[10] Selvage pits the neoliberal idea of freedom as a market principle that fosters individualism against Wallace's idea of freedom as a universally binding and collective public good. Selvage also warns of the risks to national pride and spirit posed by 'the sociological vaporings of those who talk of world states unhampered by citizenship and passports' (Selvage 1942: 2).[11]

Having set the tone for the address, he claims that public relations and advertising have become 'by force of events the

Anne Surma
Kristin
Demetrious

most important business in the country' (ibid). The responsibility of every businessman is also to practise good public relations, to 'expound his own gospel' (ibid: 3), in order to convince people that the productivity and the 'spirit' of free enterprise is of supreme importance. Selvage claims that it will, however, be the responsibility of 'skillful and intelligent publicists to unsell millions of Americans on a lot of economic tommyrot' (ibid), to counter the propaganda against enterprise delivered in the recent past. Thus, we see here how even the work of public relations is metaphorised through the language of economics and trade. As a result, it becomes possible to square the job of public relations with 'enterprise' and with 'America', as Selvage asserts:

> Our merchandise is and must be enterprise – the American system of individual initiative and profit as contrasted with a regimented economy. We are selling America itself to Americans who have forgotten what America has symbolized in the past as the envy of every other nation in the world … else freedom and its blood brother, free enterprise, will perish from the earth (ibid).

The evangelical and apocalyptic tone of the rhetoric is unmistakable, as Selvage evokes (in distilling not only public relations but American life itself to a market) what it would mean to lose the intimately connected freedom and free enterprise as a consequence of 'governmental bondage' (ibid). He also raises the question of whether public relations professionals are up to the task of winning 'the battle for free enterprise' (ibid: 9). He urges industrial executives to determine whether those public relations people they employ have 'a little pinko' (ibid: 10) in them; and to ask whether they have been out-manoeuvred by 'radicals, parlor pinks, and intellectual crackpots' (ibid: 12). Here we see Selvage using what Stedman Jones describes as 'guilt by association phraseology', which he identifies as 'a favourite tactic of the New Deal's conservative opponents', when terms such as communist or socialist were used pejoratively in describing Roosevelt's policies (2012: 142).[12]

Selvage concludes his address in combative voice by linking the power and control presently wielded by the American government with the spectre of fascism: 'And if we are going to win our fight to regain private enterprise from the stronghold of war's Fascism, then we have got to learn to hate those chains of Fascism' (1942: 13). In his ambiguous use of that term, Selvage conflates Nazi fascism with what neoliberals consider to be the fascism of interventionist government. Public relations' task, he reiterates, remains to 'cast off … our shackles and return the American people to the American Way of representative free government and honest free enterprise' (ibid). The image of shackles rather mischievously associates America's shameful slavery past with the present Roosevelt administration to suggest both the deprivation of liberty perpetrated by government and the emancipatory power of private enterprise.

Embedding discourse, transforming everyday language with plastic words

We have argued that myriad public relations efforts were instrumental in propelling and embedding the discursive impetus of the free market and free enterprise in the USA. Neoliberals from the 1930s onwards were conscious of the power of language to influence public attitudes towards and understanding of politics, government policy, not to mention people's sense of their own significance and value as human beings. Demonstrating a rationalist fervour, so convinced of its moral 'rightness' that no deliberative stance was apparently required, the writings of Selvage (and his peers, including Hazlitt, Sokolsky and Hill), as well as the organisations with which he was associated (the NAM, for example), regularly involved roundly ridiculing any idea or ideology that might suggest the connecting or integrating of the individual into a collective or community-based identity (other than a nationalism that would support individualism).

A number of features of Selvage's address above warrant further discussion, not least because they are, in different forms, to be found in the texts of his contemporaries and in those that continued to promote the ideas of neoliberalism in subsequent decades. These features are particularly significant for the ethical, communicative questions they raise. They include the deployment of a combative, oppositional rhetoric which dramatises the struggle between competing discourses for establishing the 'truth' of different domains of knowledge; the association of opponents with pejorative terms such as socialist, communist, weak or 'crackpot' (ibid: 12);[13] and the satirising of visions that assert collective, shared responsibility for improving the lives of all. However, limitations of space mean that we can only look briefly at one other feature here, and this is the practice of harnessing so-called plastic words to create an expansive vision of a future governed by the market and private enterprise. We select this feature also because it has become a ubiquitous component of contemporary vernacular language, perhaps particularly in relation to neoliberal or market-based discourse whose rhetorical precepts are today regularly accepted as natural or even normative.

The notions of free and freedom, as these are used in Selvage's text, can be analysed in relation to what Poerksen calls 'plastic words' (Plasticwörter).[14] Poerksen identifies a group of words that, though hollow or lacking precise meaning, have entered our everyday vocabulary to become accepted as 'common sense' (1995: 4). Such words include 'management', 'solution' and 'progress'. Plastic words

**Anne Surma
Kristin
Demetrious**

are modular: that is, malleable and portable. In their portability, such words become 'historically disembedded' (ibid: 22) and lose the meanings accorded by context; they are thus transformed into 'nature' (ibid: 23). Crucially, such words are typically proffered as value-free (ibid: 87). Importantly too, plastic words are general, connotative, positive terms: 'they reduce all domains to a common denominator and sound an imperative and futuristic note' (ibid: 102). While the meaning of such words as forms of knowledge is hollowed out or reduced to information bytes in their incorporation into discursive forms across institutional and public spaces, their generality often induces passivity or consensus (ibid).[15] While Poerksen's notion of plastic words is devised in the context of a globalised world, we suggest that its principles hold good in relation to the rise of neoliberal-inspired language and market discourse.

Mirowski observes that, for the neoliberals, 'market society must be treated as a "natural" and inexorable state of humankind' (Mirowski 2015: 435). Moreover, neoliberals *extol freedom as trumping all other virtues, but the definition of freedom is recoded and heavily edited within their framework*' (ibid: 437; emphasis in original). Indeed, if we look at Selvage's text we can see how the plastic words work: the rhetorical harnessing of the adjectival tag 'free' and the suitably vague abstract noun of 'freedom' are variously used to both describe and envision an unencumbered, muscular (and masculinist) nation propelled by market forces. So, for example, 'private enterprise' or 'free enterprise'[16] are repeatedly invoked as giving rise to, or as the *sine qua non* of, the 'free individual' and 'freedom' and 'free men'. In this way, market discourse can be narrated as positive, persuasive and normative. Although plastic words may appear to be value-free, this does not mean that they have no ethical significance or impact. For example, the 'free quart of milk' that Selvage refers to in his address is a misquoting of Vice-President Wallace's remark that 'the object of this war is to make it sure that everyone can have a quart of milk to drink every day' (Wallace 1942). Selvage's recasting and incorporation of the 'free' tag signifies just one, if pointed, way in which freedom comes at a cost that some simply cannot afford and do not deserve.

Who would not consent to, or embrace, freedom? Who does not want to be free? This is the appeal of plastic words: they are adaptable to the affirmative contexts into which they may be inserted. They are also, however, variously meaningful and interpretable (if we care to probe), as we see in Selvage's text where the inclusive, affirmative meanings of the term freedom may be deconstructed by its alternative applications as an exclusive privilege emphatically *not* available to all. Thus plastic words are rhetorically powerful and persuasive because they (like the discourses with which they are associated) can be de-narrativised: they can be extracted from the 'interactions between people, places and events in time' (Surma 2013: 32) and the ethical relations that bind them so that they retain some vague or generalised meaning and appear (superficially, at least) benign.

Plastic words offer an important insight into the subtle way in which effective propaganda does its work in supporting and promoting ideological agendas. Propaganda's etymological roots are found in the Latin term *propagare*, meaning to propagate (the faith). The text above reflects the evangelical pitch of Selvage's rhetoric and the way it is inflected to capture the energy, the imagination and the potential of a world governed by the free market. However, as Burgin (2012) points out, in the 1930s and early 1940s, this perspective was not broadly popular. It would take three more decades before such visionary language helped to secure a discursive stronghold in the cultural imagination of individuals, governments, institutions and corporations around the world. Nonetheless, this important communicative spade-work helped lay the ground on which the neoliberal thought collective was able to build and extend its networks over the remaining decades of the twentieth century.

Conclusion: Looking ahead – ethics and the neoliberal way

As we have shown, a key task of public relations professionals, such as Selvage, was to inscribe the discourse of the market so that it is properly positioned as the basis of all knowledge, or, in von Mises' words in *Human action*, 'the foundation upon which modern industrialism and all the moral, intellectual, technological, and therapeutical achievements of the last centuries have been built' (von Mises 1983: 885).

To date, economics, politics and history have provided the commanding perspectives on understanding neoliberalism. Yet while these disciplinary lenses are rich and insightful, we have aimed to show in this paper that there is more work to be done in understanding the complexity and contribution of the communicative work of public relations in implementing and shaping the neoliberal project. For, as Demetrious points out, practices of public relations have long sought to control contradictions in order to maintain their harmonising control over highly contested social and political issues (Demetrious 2013: 31). Unless we commit to the large task of exploring and critiquing the communicative dimensions of the neoliberal project, then we may fail to develop a more comprehensive, ethically oriented assessment of its discursive and rhetorical practices and effects and, by extension, neglect the critical task of responding meaningfully to its ongoing impacts.

Notes

[1] Philip Mirowski and Dieter Plehwe claim that 'looking for the links between experts, consultants, and other agents of implementation (think tank professionals;

Anne Surma
Kristin
Demetrious

public relations professionals) and lobby or advocacy in its various forms' is important to bridge the divide between different areas of research examining 'great transformations' (2015: xviii), such as the neoliberal project

[2] In developing *The good society*, Lippmann acknowledges the influence of 'contemporary thinkers' such British social psychologist Graham Wallas, author of *The great society* (1914), as well as von Mises and Hayek, 'whose critique of planned economy has brought a new understanding of the whole problem of collectivism'. He also acknowledges the work of John Maynard Keynes (Lippmann 2017 [1937]: xli-xlii)

[3] If Mirowski and Plehwe's significant book serves to show how the neoliberal thought collective consisted in a dynamic set of close affiliations and networks of influence, organised 'Russian Doll'-like (Mirowski 2015: 430-31), then Daniel Stedman Jones' important study, *Masters of the universe* (2012) offers a more pointedly historical, political, and transatlantic focus on the spread of neoliberal thought from the 1940s to the twenty-first century, with a specific focus on the period from 1950 to the 1980s

[4] Hazlitt's active support of the free market and his role as a central figure as a member of the neoliberal thought collective also extended well beyond the mid-1940s. As Sharon Beder (2006) points out, he helped establish the Foundation for Economic Education (FEE) in 1946, an orgnisation dedicated to advancing individual economic freedom, private property, limited government and free trade through 'economic education'. FEE is probably the earliest example of a free-market think tank, and it was a model for subsequent similar entities both in the US and internationally. Pierre Goodrich became FEE's chair, Hazlitt its vice president, von Mises was appointed its economic adviser, and Leonard Read became FEE's president and 'driving force' (Beder 2006: 45). *The Freeman* magazine, of which Hazlitt was editor in the early 1950s, was the FEE's flagship publication

[5] In 1938, Hazlitt wrote a highly favourable review of von Mises' 1922 text, *Socialism* (Hazlitt 1938) and, in 1944, a similarly positive review of Hayek's *Road to serfdom* (Hazlitt 1944)

[6] Hill provided Sokolsky with miscellaneous information for his programmes and columns, and sought Sokolsky's advice and opinion on a range of matters, for example, in relation to the Superman comic strip, which, Hill complained, 'contains more bitter denunciation of businessmen than anything I have seen outside of the "Daily Worker"' (Hill 1946)

[7] In turn, Selvage (who maintained his association with NAM) would seek Sokolsky's advice on his projects and provide him with suggestions for his writing assignments, such as a piece exposing the failures of the New Deal (Selvage 1939)

[8] That Hill was influential in activating anti-union communication rhetoric and campaigning is corroborated by Stuart Ewen (1996). He writes: 'John W. Hill – co-founder of the public relations behemoth, Hill and Knowlton – argued that a deep divide, isolating corporate management from workers and members of the general public, was the most pressing public relations problem of the day' (Ewen 1996: 358). Tedlow also points to Hill's association, not just with the free-market ideas but with the NAM: 'Thus we see the NAM supporting the Mohawk Valley Formula of Remington-Rand, or the public relations firm of Hill & Knowlton looking after the reputation of Republic Steel's Tom Girdler while he was equipping a private army, employing an extensive espionage network, and locking workers out of plants' (Tedlow 1976: 57)

[9] Selvage's support of 'the American Way' and his swipes at internationalism are evident here and throughout the presentation. See Andrew Johnstone's discussion of the role of corporate public relations (including Selvage's position), between 1938 and 1941, in America's involvement in foreign affairs (Johnstone 2017). Johnstone points out that Selvage, while deeply supportive of America First, the non-interventionist movement that lobbied against America's entry into the Second World War, refused to become associated with it officially, worried that this might lose him clients. It seems that by the time of this 1942 address, however, Selvage was less worried about making public his views

[10] Wallace situates and historicises freedom, when he says 'Men and women cannot be really free until they have plenty to eat, and time and ability to read and think and talk things over'

[11] Later in his address, Selvage derides Charlie Chaplin's vision of a post-war world without citizenship and passports (1942: 8)

[12] It is important to note that this derisory language was mobilised as a specific response to what the free market supporters regarded as the very real and looming threat of the nation's takeover by the ill-informed disseminators of dangerous left-wing ideas

[13] Angus Burgin also notes this tendency towards 'a polar understanding of economic policy and its corresponding insinuation that gradual changes in the economy led inevitably toward a dictatorial state' in Lippmann's book *The good society*, the text that marked Lippmann's 'conservative turn' (2012: 61). Burgin also asserts that 'this became the defining trope of free-market polemics in the decade that followed' (ibid: 60)

[14] In this paper, we adapt and slightly expand Poerksen's definition of plastic words (which need to fulfil 30 criteria to qualify as such; Poerksen further organises these criteria under nine broad categories) (1995: 99-103). In his account, plastic words have their origins in science (e.g. 'sexuality', 'development', 'information', 'identity', 'future', 'growth'). However, as we suggest, words such as 'free' or 'freedom' qualify as plastic words in several important respects

PAPER

[15] Today, such terms might include 'competition' or 'empowerment' or 'innovation', for example

[16] Selvage, like his peers, uses the tag 'free' interchangeably with 'private' to describe enterprise

References

Beder, Sharon (2006) *Free market missionaries: The corporate manipulation of community values*, London and New York, Earthscan

Burgin, Angus (2012) *The great persuasion: Reinventing free markets since the Depression*, Cambridge MA, Harvard University Press

Demetrious, Kristin (2013) *Public relations, activism, and social change: Speaking up*, New York and Abingdon, Oxon, Routledge

Ewen, Stuart (1996) *PR! A social history of spin*, New York, Basic Books

Fones-Wolf, Elizabeth A. (1999) Creating a favorable business climate: Corporations and radio broadcasting, 1934 to 1954, *Business History Review*, Summer, Vol. 73, No. 2 pp 221-55

Fones-Wolf, Elizabeth A. (1994) *Selling free enterprise: The business assault on labor and liberalism 1945-60*, Urbana and Chicago, University of Illinois Press

Hayek, Friedrich (1949) The intellectuals and socialism, *University of Chicago Law Review*, Vol. 16, No. 3 pp 417-433

Hazlitt, Henry (1938) A revised attack on socialism, *New York Times Book Review*, 9 January

Hazlitt, Henry (1944) An economist's view of planning, *New York Times Book Review*, 24 September p. 1

Henderson, Julie K. (2010) Come together: Rise and fall of public relations organizations in the twentieth century, *The SAGE handbook of public relations*, Heath, Robert L. (ed.) Los Angeles, SAGE Publications Inc., second edition pp 353-366

Hazlitt, Henry (1984) An interview with Henry Hazlitt, *Austrian Economics Newsletter*, Spring, Vol. 5, No. 1 pp 1-6

Hill, John W. (1946) Letter to George Sokolsky, 12 November, Box 61, Folder 15, George E Sokolsky Papers, Hoover Institution Archives

Lippmann, Walter (2017 [1937]) *The good society*. London and New York, Routledge

**Anne Surma
Kristin
Demetrious**

Manning, Selvage & Lee (2017) International directory of company histories, *Encyclopedia.com*. Available online at http://www.encyclopedia.com/books/politics-and-business-magazines/manning-selvage-lee-msl

Miller, Karen S. (1999) *Voice of business: Hill & Knowlton and postwar public relations*, Chapel Hill and London, University of North Carolina Press

Mirowski, Philip and Plehwe, Dieter (eds) (2015) *The road from Mont Pèlerin: The making of the neoliberal thought collective*, Cambridge, MA and London, Harvard University Press

Mirowski, Philip (2015) Postface: Defining neoliberalism, *The road from Mont Pèlerin: The making of the neoliberal thought collective*, Mirowski, Philip and Plehwe, Dieter (eds) Cambridge, MA and London, Harvard University Press pp 417-455

Moloney, Kevin (2006) *Rethinking public relations*, London and New York, Routledge

Phelan, Sean (2014) *Neoliberalism, media and the political*, Basingstoke, Hampshire, Palgrave Macmillan

Phillips-Fein, Kim (2015) Business conservatives and the Mont Pèlerin Society, Mirowski, Philip and Plehwe, Dieter (eds) *The road from Mont Pèlerin: The making of the neoliberal thought collective*, Cambridge, MA and London, Harvard University Press pp 280-301

Plehwe, Dieter (2015) Introduction, *The road from Mont Pèlerin: The making of the neoliberal thought collective*, Mirowski, Phillip and Plehwe, Dieter (eds) Cambridge, MA and London, Harvard University Press pp 1-42

Poerksen, Uwe (1995) *Plastic words: The tyranny of a modular language* (trans. Mason, Jutta and Cayley, David) Philadelphia, Pennsylvania University Press

Rockwell Jr, Llewellyn H. (1995) Henry Hazlitt: Journalist of the century, *Foundation for Economic Education*. Available online at https://fee.org/articles/henry-hazlitt-journalist-of-the-century/

Selvage, James P. (1942) A look ahead at public relations, New York, 4 November, Box 104, Folder 8, George E. Sokolsky Papers, Hoover Institution Archives

Selvage, James P. (1939) Letter to George Sokolsky, 25 August, Box 104, Folder 7, George E Sokolsky Papers, Hoover Institution Archives

Sriramesh, Krishnamurthy, and Vercic, Dejan (eds) (2012) *Culture and public relations: Links and implications*, London, Taylor & Francis Ltd

Stedman Jones, Daniel (2012) *Masters of the universe: Hayek, Friedman and the birth of neoliberal politics*, Princeton and Oxford, Princeton University Press

Steger, Manfred B. and Roy, Ravi K. (2010) *Neoliberalism: A very short introduction*, Oxford, Oxford University Press

Stole, Inger L. (2005) *Advertising on trial: Consumer activism and corporate public relations in the 1930s*, Urbana and Chicago, University of Illinois Press

Surma, Anne (2015) *Imagining the cosmopolitan in public and professional writing*, Basingstoke, Hampshire, Palgrave Macmillan

Tedlow, Richard S. (1976) The National Association of Manufactures and public relations during the New Deal, *Business History Review*, Spring, Vol. 50, No. 1 pp 25-45

Van Elteren, Mel (2011) *Labor and the American left: An analytical history*, Jefferson, North Carolina and London, McFarland & Company, Inc.

von Mises, Ludwig (1983) *Human action: A treatise on economics*, Greaves, Bettina Bien (ed.) Indianapolis, Liberty Fund Inc.

Wallace, Henry A. (1942) The century of the common man, 8 May, New York. Available online at http://www.americanrhetoric.com/speeches/henrywallacefreeworldassoc.htm

Note on the contributors

Anne Surma is an Associate Professor in the School of Arts at Murdoch University, in Western Australia. Her research explores the imaginative and ethical uses of discourse and rhetoric in public and professional communications. This interest is variously reflected in Anne's journal articles and chapters in edited collections, as well as in her two sole-authored books, *Public and professional writing: Ethics, imagination and rhetoric* (Palgrave Macmillan, 2005) and *Imagining the cosmopolitan in public and professional writing* (Palgrave Macmillan, 2013). She is currently working on a book-length project (with co-author Associate Professor Kristin Demetrious), contracted to OUP New York, exploring the ways in which contemporary social issues are shaped by neoliberal discourse and rhetoric. Contact details: School of Arts, Murdoch University, South Street, Murdoch, Western Australia 6150. Email: a.surma@murdoch.edu.au

Kristin Demetrious is an Associate Professor in the School of Communication and Creative Arts at Deakin University in Victoria, Australia. Kristin's research investigates power relations in public relations through a number of social sites such as activism and gender using a socio-cultural lens to explore how it (PR) can create and control forms of identity and can shape public debates that influence social directions. She has two award-winning books: monograph *Public relations, activism and social change: Speaking up* (Routledge, 2013) and an edited collection with co-author Christine Daymon: *Gender and public relations: Critical perspectives on voice, image and identity* (Routledge, 2014). Contact details: SCCA, Deakin University, Locked Bag 20000, Geelong, VIC, 3220, Australia. Email: kristin.demetrious@deakin.edu.au

PAPER

Confronting the internet's dark side: Moral and social responsibility on the free highway

Raphael Cohen-Almagor

Cambridge University Press, 2015 pp 389

ISBN 9781107513471 (paperback)

On a September morning in 2006, depressed and troubled 25-year-old Canadian Kimveer Gill drank whiskey before driving downtown to Dawson College, in Montreal, Quebec. Gill had dressed '*Matrix* style' in black combat boots, a black trench coat and armed himself with three guns. Stopping briefly at a shopping mall, he began firing an automatic weapon at random before entering the Dawson College campus where he murdered 18-year-old student Anastasia Rebecca De Sousa and injured 20 others.

One student at the college told the *Guardian*: 'I was terrified. The guy was shooting at people randomly. He didn't care, he was just shooting at everybody.' During a subsequent exchange of gunfire with police, Gill held students hostage as human shields. Eventually, after being shot in the arm himself, Gill took his own life.

The horrific incident is recounted and re-examined in some detail in *Confronting the internet's dark side* by University of Hull Professor Raphael Cohen-Almagor (pp 115-146). Shocking enough in its own right, Gill's attack has broader and perhaps equally shocking implications for a fledgling 'internet morality' – a principal theme of Cohen-Almagor's book – insofar as Montreal had been warned of its coming. For some nine months before the attack, Gill had given voice to his rage and hatred on the internet, on various blogs and in messages on his page on the notorious website, *VampireFreaks. com*, controversial for its role in several other high-profile murders (pp 118, 124).

Gill posted pictures of himself dressed in the style of his heroes from the Columbine High School shooting of April 1999 when 13 people were killed and 20 wounded (p. 118), and also expressed a desire to die 'like Romeo and Juliet, or in a hail of gunfire' (p. 117). A man 'obsessed with hate, death and guns' (p. 118), Gill wrote of 'seeking revenge' on the world for its role in his misery, even describing the weather on the day his revenge would be taken.

During all this time, police did not monitor his activities, nor did readers of *VampireFreaks.com* and the website's host, nor did the governing state alert police to a clear and imminent danger hiding in plain sight on the web. Rather, Gill enjoyed 'moral support from his website friends' who urged him on (p. 127). As we now know, mass shootings in the United States and elsewhere have only multiplied since 2006. Yet in quite a few cases the murderers had announced their intentions beforehand on the internet, whereupon little or nothing was done to stop them (p. 14). Such crimes question the role of the internet, in that it provides spaces for unfettered freedom of expression (p. 59) and of the effectiveness of various codes of conduct for Internet Service Providers (pp 162-165).

Furthermore, what moral and social responsibility is incumbent upon those who become aware of such threats, but do not act? For instance, those who knew of, or might have surmised, Gill's intent? At the broader level there is a proven link between violent video games and violent crime, but the knowledge does not stop their production and distribution, nor does it diminish their popularity with players such as Gill who confessed to liking *Super Columbine Massacre RPG*, released in 2005 (p. 121).

As Cohen-Almagor unflinchingly notes: 'On the internet, people exchange fantasies of how they would like to violently rape and murder young girls. On a webpage called "Place of dark desires", people can watch rape videos, some of which show the raping of pre-teen girls' (p. 115).

When the internet first appeared in the public sphere in the 1990s, it was touted as a utopia that subverted mainstream thinking, a place where unrestricted freedom of speech could flourish. Its promise was that scholars, lawmakers, teachers and teens could all engage equally in a non-stop global conversation. To an extent that has come true, and the internet has changed the way we study, shop, travel, stay in touch and entertain ourselves. It encourages freedom of communication, expression and creativity and, through emergent virtual reality technologies, is even reshaping the way some users perceive the world. Despite its benefits, however, the web has a darker side where lawmakers struggle to shine a light. There lurks a dangerous ambiguity, a Jekyll and Hyde binarism evident most readily perhaps in social networking. Networking services like Facebook and Twitter are both hugely popular and valuable, yet simultaneously troubled and, at times, seemingly demonic in the vile chatter they foster and permit.

With the promise of a platform for every voice, social media works night and day to extol but, at the same time, undermine the freedom of speech it claims as a birthright. More than 40 per cent of the world's population is online; that is more than three billion people (p. 4). But cyber bullying, hate speech, trolling, call it what you will: the purveyors of hate are now a widely identified species inhabiting online ecosystems. And they are found in equal numbers on the left and right of the political spectrum. Regulating such a diffuse and intangible space, one that reaches transnationally across traditional politico-legal, ethical and moral boundaries, is a perplexing proposition, one researchers tend to conclude is 'very difficult – some say virtually impossible' (p. 3). Nonetheless, Cohen-Almagor tackles the challenge of regulating the internet head on, making extensive use of case studies to discuss the issues of 'moral and social responsibility'.

He argues it is past 'time to start a discussion in the realm of morality and ethics' to supplement 'discussions in the realm of law' (p. 11). For without clear directions for growth, the internet risks becoming a dangerous runaway we cannot rein in. 'The hurried acceptance of the internet in the Western world has been accompanied by the controversial realization that no central authority sets standards for acceptable content on this network,' he writes (p. 5).

Indeed, tucked away behind the internet's many virtues are 'direct and specific calls for murder, child pornography, direct calls for terrorism and spreading of electronic viruses, and material protected by copyright legislation' (pp 3-4). But unexpected consequences arising from technology are nothing new, since 'throughout history, each major innovation in communication has caused distress and confusion similar to what the world is experiencing today with the internet' (p. 308).

But how to match the internet's speed of growth to society's best interests? Cohen-Almagor argues the internet itself is 'not the problem', proposing, instead, that problems arise only where the internet is used to undermine our well-being as autonomous beings in free societies (p. 11). The book's first three chapters give historical, technical and theoretical context. Chapter One provides a valuable and highly readable history reaching from the mere glimmer of a US internet in the shadow of Sputnik, to the global networks of the present day. Technophobes will find the technical framework of Chapter Two handy for explaining a basic web vernacular, from terms such as 'packet' (a small bundle of data coded into zeroes and ones), to the gentle art of 'packet switching' (a nifty electronic mechanism without which the internet would not have launched).

Chapter Three leans heavily on the work of Luciano Floridi who calls the age of the internet a 'fourth scientific revolution' (p. 49) and explores the interrelated notions of answerability, accountability and social responsibility. Such ideas are manifest, for example, in the development of systems for the user-rating of a web service or product and designed to promote trust in the service or product (p. 51).

Bearing in mind that anyone may upload information to the internet, ideas of trust are similarly crucial to assessing the value of any material found online, prompting Cohen-Almagor to formulate a multi-tiered trust framework for evaluating sources (pp 65-73) and to distinguish between legal, moral and social responsibility in meeting such expectations of trust. Two theories, of 'the democratic catch' and 'moral panics', are introduced in an effort to strike a balance between protecting democracy and maintaining respect for liberal values.

Later chapters examine the responsibilities of various internet stakeholders. Chapter Four introduces the netcitizen, implying a netuser with a moral compass, while Chapter Five examines the role of the reader and how they might (or should) react when encountering anti-social speech or material (a discussion based closely around the Kimveer Gill case). Chapters Six and Seven examine ISPs and web-hosting services which have a social responsibility not only for their own content but for content provided by third parties – an increasingly difficult ask in a media landscape boasting no borders in a world dogged by terrorism, child pornography, cybercrime, hate speech and cyber bullying.

Chapter Eight probes the role of the state in monitoring violations of law and the public interest and, as regulator, in protecting vulnerable minorities. This chapter also reviews current provisions globally and provides several interesting case studies under the edict that 'governments have a moral duty to intervene to enforce their customary moral norms of the day'. For example, the court case over Yahoo being asked to cease or block the sale of Nazi memorabilia from its American websites, a practice illegal in France but allowed in the US (p. 231). And finally, international cooperation and the steps already taken towards binding agreements are discussed in Chapter Eight, such as the Council of Europe's 2001 Convention on Cybercrime (p. 277). In the Conclusion, the book makes a raft of recommendations (pp 312-315), including pragmatic suggestions, such as that the National Centre for Missing and Exploited Children (NCMEC) share its image data bank with all ISPs and that the ISPs share theirs back and with each other. Cohen-Almagor also proposes a new browser he calls CleaNet which would be free of government ties, perhaps philanthropically funded. In fact, the vision of a socially responsible browser-for-the-age emulates an Athenian-style democracy, where each participant has an equal voice in its conception, planning and operation. Exactly how CleaNet might be planned, launched and governed runs to seven pages of remarkable detail, including the suggestion that its vetting and censorship role be steered by a committee of between 100 to 400 netcitizens.

Undoubtedly a bold vision, CleaNet's management structure might, nonetheless, appear to be unwieldy, if not problematic. But *Confronting the internet's dark side* can rightfully claim to be a first: a thought-provoking, rigorously researched and consistently critical journey across the internet's moral and ethical landscapes, and one that arrives just in the nick of time.

Generous footnotes, a useful glossary, bibliography and index accompany a book that is readable as a general reference for researchers and would make a valuable addition to any university or public library, or as a text in schools of media, communications, cultural studies, law and philosophy.

Doubtless some will continue to argue the internet's lack of regulation is its greatest asset. But we would do well to heed Cohen-Almagor's warning to weigh freedom of expression against social responsibility. In all areas of human life and endeavour, we accept boundaries that allow our societies to function. Such regulation helps define who we are and where we want to go. Dignity, moral worth and an imperative to 'do no harm' are our companions in the real world. Why not on the internet?

Dr Glenn Morrison,
Tutor in Writing and Cultural Studies,
Charles Darwin University, Alice Springs Campus

Literary journalism and the aesthetics of experience
John C. Hartsock

University of Massachusetts Press, 2016 pp 195
ISBN 9781625341747 (paperback)

John C. Hartsock, Professor of Communication Studies at the State University of New York at Cortland and author of the seminal *A history of American literary journalism* (2000), has produced a masterful new text that deepens and expounds upon his previous arguments. Hartsock claims that narrative literary journalism, which he defines as 'a journalism that emphasizes narrative and descriptive modalities' (p. 3), constitutes a genre distinctive from newspaper reportage, memoir, fiction and more traditional journalism. He traces the use of this term back to the early 20th century, identifying James Agee's *Let us now praise famous men* (1941) on through Tom Wolfe's edited collection of reportage, *New Journalism* (1973), as well as other international manifestations such as the Russian *ocherk*, the Chinese *baogao wenxue* and the Colombian *nuevo periodismo*.

REVIEW

Hartsock contextualises narrative literary journalism within both the context of the American tradition of more fact-based and objective journalism as well as through using the tools and techniques available to fiction-writers. While both forms foreground the use of storytelling as a narrative device, literary journalism provides readers with an 'aesthetics of experience' (p. 4) revealing 'our phenomenal world, one that is conjured imaginatively by means of sensate experiences reflected in language'. Rather than connoting something either historical or beautiful, the sense of the aesthetics for Hartsock reflects 'phenomenal experience that prompts a sensory response'.

Hartsock then proceeds to differentiate narrative literary journalism (or what he also calls 'narra-descriptive journalism') from what we deem hard news by referring to the model of the 'inverted pyramid' (p. 10) so endemic in the latter; in traditional 'objective' journalism, the conclusion of a story and its most important aspects will often come at the beginning in what's called a 'summary lead' and will move on to the least relevant information at the end. However, in narrative literary journalism, Hartsock argues, this model has less bearing because the rhetorical exposition can be much more complex, digressive and provide the sort of climax or resolution that we may find in a novel.

To support his arguments, Hartsock calls upon theorists such as the Russian literary critics, Mikhail Bakhtin and Viktor Shklovsky. He is particularly interested in Bakhtin's concept of the chronotope (p. 28), or how different literary genres engage distinctive configurations of space and time, which gives those genres their salient narrative character. Narrative literary journalism, he claims, embodies a dynamic process that is 'both phenomenal and linguistic' (p. 29) in nature and where the narrative is inseparable from the evidence of a precise time place; whereas in the strictly fictional, there is an indirect or allegorical relationship between these elements. This form allows for the epistemological instability and temporal complexity of reality that counter certain habituated modes of perception perpetuated by other genres of writing. Hartsock is also interested in how narrative literary journalism employs Shklovsky's idea of *ostranenie* (p. 34), or defamiliarisation, by which the familiar is made strange, thereby providing us with new insights about the real world.

Using the example of Hunter S. Thompson's 'gonzo journalism', as well as works such as Truman Capote's *In cold blood*, John Hersey's *Hiroshima*, Joan Didion's *Slouching towards Bethlehem* and Michael Herr's *Dispatches*, Hartsock makes a compelling argument for the distinctive quality of narra-descriptive journalism, especially in the way such work subverts the myth and the symbolism of novels, while also simultaneously being more elastic and multifaceted than conventional journalism.

Hartsock's new book is a brilliant and wide-ranging discussion, drawing parallels between literary narrative journalism and quantum physics (or how the observer changes the observed), while bringing in Roland Barthes on mythology, Walter Benjamin on 'factography' and Friedrich Nietzsche's idea of *qualitas occulta* (or the way ideological abstractions obviate the 'differentiating qualities of individual phenomena [or] persons' (p. 31)).

In short, Hartsock makes a strong case for the necessity of this form of writing and storytelling, particularly in the world of new media and an era of diminishing reading capabilities.

Ravi Shankar,
The University of Sydney

Covering conflict: The making and unmaking of new militarism

Richard Lance Keeble

Bury St Edmunds, Suffolk, Abramis, 2017 pp 367

ISBN 9781845497101 (paperback)

Richard Lance Keeble has written a book about the anti-democratic, frequently deceptive 'military/industrial/intelligence/media complex' (p. 2). A second, updating edition of one of his previous books, *Secret state, silent press*, of 1997 (p. 1), the book is more a critique of the underlying structures of mass media and journalism than it is of individual journalists, many of whom do a fine job within the limits imposed upon them by the nature of the mass market and, of course, the secret state. By 1990, the UK had more than 100 laws prohibiting the disclosure of supposedly sensitive information, making it one of the most secretive states in the word (p. 23).

Keeble's book is as much, perhaps more, about omission in mainstream media as it is about content: for instance, the lack of the coverage of underlying causes of war and of civilian casualties. This creates a framework in which power is unaccountable and government decisions are undemocratic.

In Chapter One, Keeble argues that the 'old' militarism was conscription-based. But, with the triumph of the Labour Party after World War Two, and, perhaps more importantly, the acquisition of nuclear weapons by the UK and US, a 'new' militarism gradually emerged. Private media, linked in various ways to the deep state, smeared any moves from sectors of the public and the Labour Party (then under Michael Foot) towards unilateral nuclear disarmament (p. 19).

As British institutions appeared to become more democratic, the military, particularly in light of its new high-tech developments putting humans increasingly out of the loop, became more secretive. Parallel to these developments was the evolution in media of war as a spectacle. Perhaps the most important development was the manufacturing via institutional structures of faux audience participation. By this, Keeble (pp 7-8) refers to the 'live' nature of war coverage thanks to satellite television, as pioneered during the coverage of the Gulf War 1991. As secrecy intensified, commercial secrecy in the international arms trade, where Britain was and remains a big player, also grew (pp 18-19). Keeble argues that the state 'was seen as vulnerable to threat from technological advances within the media. In the event, the US invasions of the 1980s culminating in the attack on Iraq, showed that the new media technologies were, in fact, highly vulnerable to manipulation by the state' (p. 14).

Chapter Two concerns journalists and the secret state. In this chapter, Keeble, careful to emphasise that the security state is not monolithic, reviews the deep state nexus, documenting the incestuous connections of the police, military police forces, special forces, foreign intelligence agencies and the infrastructure that holds them together. Keeble then goes on to discuss those journalists who are connected in one way or the other to the intelligence services. Keeble's subchapter on what he calls the 'conspiracy theory conundrum' (p. 65) argues that the entire military-industrial-media complex operates to a significant extent on conspiracy. Yet when researchers 'highlight its significance [they are] accused of lacking academic rigour and promoting "conspiracy theory"'. Keeble concludes, cautiously, that 'conspiratorial elements have to be acknowledged' at times, when discussing media and war reporting.

Chapter Three concerns what Keeble calls an emergence of a new militarist consensus. There was a near-consensus against war in the US among the general public but, as Keeble notes, the public has become increasingly alienated from the workings of the state, due in part to the media. By the time of the Gulf War 1991, coverage had changed to distance audiences at home from the horror of carpet bombing (or 'precision bombing' in the propaganda nomenclature) abroad. In the UK, the Labour government under Jim Callaghan had prepared for an invasion of the Falklands Islands/Malvinas by Argentina (which claims the islands as its rightful, post-colonial territory) as early as 1977. The Falklands War of 1982 'set a hugely significant precedent', writes Keeble (p. 93), helping in the creation of a 'permanent war economy' (p. 95). Photographs, film and reports were deliberately delayed by the military, correspondents were embedded in heavily controlled pools with the armed forces while other journalists were blacklisted.

In Chapter Four, Keeble studies the cases of the US's Grenada invasion of 1983 and the 'Irangate' scandal of 1985-1987. The idea that instant global communication allows unprecedented, uncensored access to war coverage is a myth, he suggests. In Grenada, a carefully managed media campaign succeeded in covering up the number of casualties, presenting the invasion as an instant response to alleged transgressions, exaggerating the threat of Grenada to US interests and selling the war to the American public with a 71 per cent approval rating. 'Irangate' or the Iran-Contra Affair, involved elements of the US military illegally selling arms, via conduits in Israel, to Iran, one of America's official enemies, to fund its illegal activities in Nicaragua. The Pentagon-led media strategy over so-called Low Intensity Conflict 'prioritised covert warfare' (p. 121), making journalistic investigations very difficult. Interestingly, no significant investigation, both at the media or governmental levels, followed the revelations of the foreign editor of Hearst newspapers, John Wallach, concerning 'Irangate' in June 1985. It was only after a Lebanese newspaper reported on the events in November 1986 that the international media chased the story.

In Chapter Five, Keeble argues that the new militarism, being contingent on public ignorance of Third World dynamics, sought to portray Saddam Hussein, the dictator of Iraq, as a villain in a simplistic struggle between good and evil. When Saddam was an ally of the US and Great Britain during the 1980s, media coverage of his atrocities was 'restrained' (p. 128). Keeble gives the example of Halabja 1988, when 5,000 Kurds were slaughtered. 'Little blame was levelled personally at Saddam Hussein in the press' (ibid). When Saddam became the enemy, he was rapidly labelled 'Hitler' (p. 134).

Chapter Six highlights the lack of media questioning concerning the motives for supporting dictators and arms sales, and in waging war. Sticking with the example of the Gulf War 1991, Keeble notes that few reports of the period asked what the war was really all about. The veneer painted by the media was that of Saddam raving against Kuwait for stealing Iraq's oil and blaming US allies for driving down oil prices. A deeper context is imperialism, particularly British, given the UK's role in the war. Keeble goes on to note 'secret' wars (i.e., those ignored or marginalised in the corporate media) in the decades leading up to the Gulf War. These include Oman (1968-1977) and the inevitable collusion with the expanding US empire.

In Chapter Seven, Keeble argues that the media shaped public opinion about war in several ways. After Iraq invaded Kuwait in August 1990, 'Most of the press had no time for talk – they wanted war and right now' (p. 165). The tabloids' warmongering was predictable. But what were the motivations of the so-called left-leaning press? Keeble quotes the *Guardian*'s then-principal feature writer, Martin Woollacott, who says that his colleagues were divided over how to cover the war, referring to diplomacy versus military action. By the end of August 1990, however, the majority of *Independent* articles supported war. Keeble then goes on to document how newspapers sought to exclude critical voices. On the manipulation of public opinion, the supposedly more liberal media constructed polls as to avoid the option of peace negotiations and even asked the public if they would support assassinating Saddam (p. 176).

Chapter Eight concerns the modes of censorship employed by the Ministry of Defence and the media itself in (mis)reporting the war. Correspondents were 'pooled' in hotels and carefully managed by the US military. 'The highest contingents in the press corps' were American and British (p. 184). The non-pooled journalists were expected to stay in hotels. Learning their lessons of embedding in the Falklands War, direct censorship was not needed because journalists had 'bonded' (p. 191) with their military counterparts and were thus less likely to write critically about them.

Returning to the theme of high-tech war, as ushered in by the nuclear age, Chapter Nine traces the history of 'nukespeak' (Chilton quoted on p. 198) to the development of so-called high-precision weapons as used in the Gulf War 1991. Coupled with the other factors analysed in previous chapters, the media's handling of high-tech weapons further sought to dehumanise Iraqis.

Chapter Ten argues that the casualty disparity between the allied forces and the Iraqi forces was so large that it was not really a 'war': more a series of massacres of a largely defenceless 'enemy'. On the occasion that civilian atrocity stories did make it to print or television, the mantra was to blame Saddam Hussein.

Chapter Eleven moves on from the Middle East and into Somalia and Yugoslavia. As the United States launched Operation Restore Hope in 1992, supposedly to end a famine which was ending anyway, the US government ensured its business relations with US energy giants operating in the country remained secure. In Serbia in 1999, NATO launched a supposed humanitarian war to save Kosovar Albanians, some of whom (such as the Kosovo Liberation Army) were linked to al-Qaeda and trained by US and British forces. In defence of the KLA, the US-led NATO bombed Serbia, preparing the way for the independence of Kosovo nearly a decade later in 2008. Just as the US blamed Saddam for US-led atrocities in Iraq, Serbia's President Milošević was blamed for what NATO did to his country.

In Chapter Twelve, Keeble argues that the Gulf War of 2003 was a 'myth' (p. 265): the threat posed by Saddam and his supposed Weapons of Mass Destruction was almost entirely a fabrication, the Iraqi armed forces collapsed quickly, and massive fire-power ('shock and awe') quickly destroyed the civilian infrastructure. Media management was essentially a repeat of the Gulf War 1991 and Serbia 1999: the Pentagon devised a large-scale (dis)information campaign, the secret state operated without public or media oversight and, disturbingly, the number of Western journalists killed in the war reached 15.

The concluding Chapter Thirteen is unusual in that it criticises the pretext for war in Afghanistan in 2001: something that many scholars, including those critical of the invasion of Iraq 2003, failed to do. The war script – a deadly enemy, precision weapons, etc – was rehashed, this time to more effect than in previous conflicts due to the then-recent 9/11 atrocities which convinced most Britons and Americans that al-Qaeda in Afghanistan, together with their

Taliban sponsors, must be destroyed. As the US-British occupation continued, the enemy used ever-deadly methods of resistance against the occupiers, or terrorism as Western media called it. These included suicide bombings and improvised explosive devices. In 2010, Britain and France signed a defence cooperation treaty. Within a year, both countries joined the US via NATO in destroying Libya. Keeble also deals with the 2013 war, led by France, against elements operating in Mali.

In the Conclusion, Keeble summarises the grim reality of war: civilian casualties, soldier casualties, and financial expenditure, which could have been invested in more progressive programmes at home. The high-tech, highly-controlled informational nature of the so-called new militarism has morphed into 'disaster militarism' (p. 315).

REVIEW

Keeble's book balances accessibility with scholarly rigour. It is an important contribution to the literature concerning media coverage of conflict and the growth of an increasingly out-of-control security state.

Dr T. J. Coles is a postdoctoral researcher at Plymouth University's Cognition Institute, and the author of several books, including *Britain's secret wars* and *Fire and fury* (both Clairview Books). His latest, *Human wrongs* (Iff Books), is due to be published later this year

Peter Preston: 'Great wordsmith'

Preston, editor of the *Guardian* for almost 20 years from 1975 who has died aged 79, was not just a great writer and journalist but a totally reliable one too, writes John Mair. I have now edited twenty two books on matters journalistic. The latest, *Brexit, Trump and the media*, was published late last year. Peter's contributions were a cornerstone of more than half of them over the last decade. He wrote always brilliantly, always eloquently, always willingly.

The process is simple. – I (and others) invent a topic to cover: for instance, phone hacking, Leveson, the death of print, the putative death of the BBC or Channel Four. We then invite a cast of authors to contribute.

Peter was always *primus inter pares*: – our first port of call. He had an open invitation and always chose his own furrow to plough on the subject under investigation. It was always original.

Peter did not really need an editor in advance nor any subbing after. He was self-editing. He always delivered his copy pasted on an email, never in a Word document. Every word was a gem, carefully chosen, every idea original, all worthy reading. We could ask for no more.

Our Abramis 'hackademic' series is much enriched by the writings of Peter Preston. Farewell great wordsmith. We shall miss you.

Robert Parry: 'A brilliant investigative reporter'

Robert Parry, editor and publisher of the leading US-based investigative site, *Consortiumnews.com*, has died aged 68, writes Richard Lance Keeble.

Parry and his colleague Brian Barger were the first journalists in 1985 to report on the illegal US arms shipments to Iran alongside a cocaine trafficking operation by the Nicaraguan contras – all backed by the Reagan administration and the CIA. It became the subject of a congressional investigation led by then-Senator John Kerry (D-Mass.) in 1986.

His next big scoop came with his 'October Surprise' revelations. Following the release of 52 American hostages in Tehran moments after Ronald Reagan was sworn in as president on 20 January 1981, suspicions grew that there had been some sort of deal agreed between the Reagan campaign and the Iranians. But it wasn't until Parry uncovered a trove of documents in a House of Representatives office building basement in 1994 that the evidence became overwhelming that the Reagan campaign had, indeed, interfered with the Carter administration's efforts to free the hostages before the 1980 election.

Launching *Consortiumnews.com* in the mid-1990s, Parry backed the publication in 1996 of Gary Webb's 'Dark Alliance' series of reports in the *San Jose Mercury-News*. Webb's series reopened the contra-cocaine controversy with a detailed examination of the drug trafficking networks in Nicaragua and Los Angeles that had helped to spread highly addictive crack cocaine across the United States. Webb, however, faced vitriolic attacks from corporate newspapers such as the *Washington Post*, *New York Times* and *Los Angeles Times* – and in 2004, aged just 49, committed suicide. In his memory, Parry and the board of directors for the Consortium for Independent Journalism launched the Gary Webb Freedom of the Press Award in 2015.

Following 9/11, the website provided a home for voices that questioned the case for invading Iraq in 2003. Former CIA analyst Ray McGovern and some of his colleagues founded Veteran Intelligence Professionals for Sanity and established a long-running relationship with *Consortiumnews*. As his son Nat Parry wrote in a tribute to his father, 'several former intelligence veterans began contributing to the website, motivated by the same independent spirit of truth-telling that compelled Bob to invest so much in this project'.

Parry also featured prominently in Oliver Stone's 2016 documentary *Ukraine on fire* where he showed how US-funded NGOs and media companies had worked with the CIA and foreign policy establishment since the 1980s to promote the US geopolitical agenda.

Also in 2016, *Consortiumnews.com* was blacklisted (along with 200 other websites) on a website called *PropOrNot* which claimed to serve as a watchdog against undue 'Russian influence' in the United States. *PropOrNot* was even elevated by the *Washington Post* as a credible source, though it hid behind a cloak of anonymity. Last year, Parry won the Martha Gellhorn Prize for Journalism.

The veteran investigative reporter, John Pilger, said he 'was a beacon of principled, often courageous journalism in a landscape of compliant, distorted anti-journalism.' And Richard Lance Keeble, joint editor of *Ethical Space*, commented: 'Robert Parry was a brilliant and brave investigative journalist: a voice of sanity amidst the madness of America – dominated as it is by its military/industrial/ intelligence/media complex.'

- See https://consortiumnews.com/2018/01/28/robert-parrys-legacy-and-the-future-of-consortiumnews/

The Institute of Communication Ethics

ICE aims to:

- formalise the study and practice in the fast growing discipline of CE and articulate the communication industries' concerns with ethical reasoning and outcomes;

- provide communication practitioners with a centre to drive the study of ethical practice in communications;

- develop specific tools, quality frameworks and training methods and provide them to its members; assess initiatives in related disciplines and offer guidance and ethics training for communicators;

- offer qualifications that support the practice of communication as an ethical discipline underpinned by principles, rules of conduct and systematic self-examination.

Membership Application

I would like to apply for annual membership to the ICE with:

☐ Personal membership with access to Ethical Space online (£55)

☐ Personal membership plus printed copy of Ethical Space (£75)

☐ Organisational membership (non profit £200, for profit (small) £500, multinational £5000)

Note: Please contact the ICE office for further details of local chapters of ICE.

Name _____

Address _____

Country _____ Postcode _____

Email _____

Tel _____ Fax _____

Name of University/Institute/Organisation _____

Payment

☐ I enclose a cheque payable to 'Institute of Communication Ethics'

Please return to:

Dr Fiona Thompson, 69 Glenview Road, Nab Wood, Shopley, West Yorkshire, BD18 4AR

For assistance please contact: info@communication-ethics.net

Lightning Source UK Ltd.
Milton Keynes UK
UKOW05f0020090218

317598UK00005B/331/P